Amazing Animals
of the World

Written by Anne McKie
Illustrated by Ken McKie

© 1999 Grandreams Limited

Published by Grandreams Limited
435-437 Edgware Road
Little Venice, London W2 1TH

Printed in Indonesia

CONTENTS

INTRODUCING AMAZING ANIMALS...

There is a magnificent variety of wildlife on this planet.

We share the Earth with over one million species of insects, 8,800 different sorts of birds and 4,500 kinds of mammals.

Many creatures are able to survive in scorching dry deserts, others survive in snow and ice with temperatures below freezing all the year round. Some spend their whole lives in the sea, while others live in jungles and tropical rainforests.

Sadly, much of the world's wildlife is in danger of being lost forever. Man is destroying the planet's rainforests at an alarming rate. All of us must work together to protect every living creature and its habitat. Let's start exploring this wildlife with a look at one of the most feared families – the bear!

THE BEARS

The fishing bear

Grizzly bears love fish and congregate in and around rivers and streams when the salmon are spawning and leaping out of the water.

When grizzlies catch salmon, they strip off the flesh very carefully from either side, and leave behind the bones, the head and the tail.

These bears feed mostly on berries and dig up roots and tubers – often eating up to 16 kilograms (35 lb) of plants a day. The grizzly also eats grubs and mice, young deer, and of course, salmon!

The five sharp claws on a grizzly bear's front paws are 6 centimetres (2.4 in) long – very useful for digging up food and climbing. No wonder they are always hungry – these bears can measure up to 2.8 metres (9 ft)!

The big and the small

The polar bear is the biggest bear of all. It weighs about 20 times more than the smallest species, the sun bear, which averages about 36 kilograms (80 lb).

The grizzly bear

Grizzlies weigh almost half a ton, but they don't always lumber along! When provoked, they can charge at 64 kilometres per hour (40 mph). Although male grizzlies can fight with a rival bear to the death, they rarely attack humans. They have very poor eyesight and could mistake a person for another bear. This solitary creature is becoming rare and endangered in many parts of North America.

The Kodiak bear

There are around 3,000 of these brown bears living on Kodiak Island off Alaska... and they are BIG!

Although the prize for the largest bear goes to the polar bear, the Kodiak is the most heavily built brown bear. A large male can weigh as much as 600 kilograms (1,323 lb). These bears grow so huge because there is plenty of food available on the island.

The polar bear

This gigantic bear is the largest living carnivore. It is the biggest of all the bears and can measure 3.3 metres (11 ft) from nose to tail, and weigh up to 750 kilograms (1,654 lb).

Thick white fur and a layer of fat protects polar bears from the bitter Arctic cold and icy water, as they often swim for hours at a time between pack ice and land.

The American black bear

These bears hibernate for as long as seven months in one year. They live in forests where they feed on berries, nuts, bulbs and grubs. They are very fond of honey!

Black bears are known for begging from campers, people picnicking and cars visiting national parks. They can become very dangerous if denied food!

The sloth bear

This bear found in India can hang upside down with its long curved claws – just like a sloth!

When feeding on termites, the sloth bear forms its lips and tongue into a tube shape, then sucks up a snack!

The sun bear

The sun bear of Southeast Asia is the smallest of all the bears, measuring up to 1.2 metres (4 ft) in length. It gets its name from the patch of yellowish fur on its chest.

The sun bear's claws open termite mounds with ease, enabling it to scoop out tasty insects with its long tongue.

The bear with spectacles

The spectacled bear from South America, with its rim of white fur around the eyes, really looks as though it is wearing glasses! This bear lives in humid forests, climbing trees to reach fruit and the fleshy centres of plants. It measures 1.8 metres (6 ft) long and can weigh up to 114 kilograms (250 lb).

The moon bear

This Asian black bear is also called a 'moon bear' because of the half circle of white hair on its chest, rather like a crescent moon. It has a shaggy mane of long hair round its neck.

Bear facts

Polar bears are not endangered; 25-45,000 live in the Arctic.

The Inuit (people of the Arctic) word for 'bear' is 'nanuk'.

Polar bears are excellent long-distance swimmers, travelling more than 100 kilometres (62 mi) in one lengthy swim.

Underneath a polar bear's white coat is a black skin.

In spring a Kodiak bear can eat up to 20 salmon a day. When it comes out of its winter den, the Kodiak has a BIG appetite!

The American black bear is the most common of all the bears... it is thought there could be over a quarter of a million.

A grizzly bear is tiny at birth, weighing less than 45 kilograms (99 lb). There are usually three or four cubs in a litter.

You can tell how old a bear is by counting the number of rings in one of its teeth – a bit like counting the ring of a tree trunk. Of course this is very dangerous and you must not try it out!

Grizzlies can live up to 30 years in the wild and over 45 in captivity.

For the American black bear, black is not the only colour. They come in brown, blue-black and cinnamon. There is even a white 'black bear'!

FASCINATING FACTS

Pussycat Pilgrims

The first short-haired cats were taken to North America by the Pilgrim Fathers in 1620. The *Mayflower* sailed from Plymouth, England carrying 102 settlers, numerous cats, dogs, pigs, goats, sheep, poultry and rabbits. They arrived in Plymouth, Massachusetts after a 65-day voyage.

An after-dinner snooze

Sometimes when a vampire bat has had a good meal, it has to relax and take it easy for a while. The bat has often drunk so much blood it can't take off! It has to wait until some of the meal has been digested and passed through its system.

Birds beware!

It looks just like an ordinary snail, but it is doubtful if the birds in your garden would dare fly down and eat one!

The African giant land snail is enormous. Its shell is about 20 centimetres (8 in) long and its body can measure up to 39 centimetres (15 in).

African giant land snail

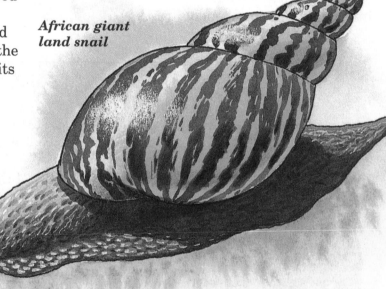

Keep quite still!

A rhinoceros cannot see you if you are more than 30 metres (100 ft) away, provided you keep very still. They have poor vision and their eyes are set back on either side of their head. But they do have very good hearing and an excellent sense of smell.... so get ready to run!

10

The animal in your bath!

Did you know that there is an animal in the bath beside you... the sponge! In the ocean, sponges stay in one place and feed in a very simple way. Sea water is filtered through the thousands of tiny holes in the sponge, and any food particles are left behind for the sponge to enjoy!

Sea sponge

Baby bills

The bills of young toucans are rather dull and small... not a bit like their colourful parents. As the young birds grow, their bills become bigger and brighter.

Old Red Eyes

An American lizard, better known as the horned toad, can shoot a 1.8 metre (6 ft) blast of blood through a sinus at the bottom of its eyelid when disturbed.

Argali sheep

What a headache!

The argali sheep is the largest wild sheep of all. It lives in the mountains and cold regions of Central Asia. Its huge curved horns can weigh as much as 22.6 kilograms (50 lb)... enough to give anyone a headache!

BELIEVE IT OR NOT

How did the grizzly bear get its name?

Grizzly bears are sometimes aggressive and bad-tempered, but that is not the reason why they are called 'grizzly'.

These bears get their name from the creamy-grey ends of their fur, which make it look matted or grizzled.

Pandas are party animals

Nothing could be further from the truth. Pandas are shy and solitary and don't appear to like the company of other pandas at all. Zoos have had very little success with breeding, and this may be one reason why.

Do ostriches bury their heads in the sand?

Although ostriches do the strangest things, this famous saying is not true! But here is one strange truth... an ostrich will swallow almost anything – nuts and bolts, stones, pieces of wire, small tools left lying around and even wrist watches!

Ostriches do, however, sit with their necks and heads resting on the ground, which may have given rise to the rumour that ostriches bury their heads in the sand.

Flying fish spotted from jumbo jets!

The fins of flying fish can be used rather like wings, but these little fish don't actually fly – they glide. Flying fish speed through the water, then as they leap out they fly through the air up to 6 metres (20 ft) high... which is a bit low to be seen by passengers in a jumbo jet!

Frogmouths live on frogs

This bird, which looks rather like a nightjar, has a wide gaping mouth. Frogmouths hunt at night and pounce on their prey from the ground or a low branch. They gobble up snails, centipedes, scorpions, and of course, lots of FROGS!

Do humpback whales sing in a chorus?

They would make a lovely sound if they did! But unfortunately this isn't true. The humpback whale sings its melody alone, sometimes for over half an hour. This is how whales keep in touch with each other, often when they are over a hundred kilometres apart.

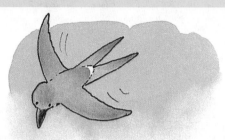

Saliva soup is on the menu

In China, bird's nest soup is a very expensive delicacy. The main ingredient is the nest of a swift, made of twigs and other forest debris that the bird cements together with its sticky saliva... yuk!

Are all snakes in Ireland green?

Trick question! Believe it or not, there are no snakes in Ireland! Legend has it that St. Patrick, the country's patron saint, banished snakes over 1,600 years ago because he thought they were evil!

Polly-grip

Some parrots have beaks that are so strong, they use them to pull themselves up tree trunks... so watch your fingers when a parrot is around!

Migrating birds go on a diet?

Before they set off to fly great distances, birds must put on weight, not lose it! They must eat more to build up reserves of fat for the journey. Small birds often double their weight.

A fox can cover his tracks

Some people once believed that the red fox swept away its tracks in the snow with its long bushy tail. Foxes are known to be sly and cunning, but they're not that clever!

Professor Polly

Parrots are clever creatures – those kept as pets will often mimic their human keepers.

THE BIG CATS OF AFRICA

The king of beasts

Lions are social animals. They are the only cats that live and hunt together in groups.

A group of lions, called a pride, consists of about 5-15 related lionesses, their offspring and up to six adult males. The lionesses do most of the hunting while the lions protect the pride from rival males and defend the group's territory... and all the adults help to look after and bring up each other's cubs.

A big male lion can weigh up to 240 kilograms (530 lb) – twice as much as some of the females. Nose to tail, a male can measure a massive 3.3 metres (10.8 ft) in length! The loud roaring of a lion can be heard up to 5 kilometres (3 mi) away.

A lion's shaggy mane makes it look bigger, and in a fight the mane protects the lion's neck and head.

Leopard

All by itself

The leopard is a solitary animal, spending much of its time in trees. Leopards hunt alone by night; they do not chase or stalk their prey, but lie in wait, then pounce on their victim.

Sometimes a leopard will wait high up in the branches of a tree until an animal is passing below. Then it will drop down onto the unsuspecting prey, kill it, then drag it back up the tree to eat undisturbed by any other scavengers.

The black panther

It was once thought that the black panther was a separate species. Now we know that this legendary animal is really a black-coated leopard.

The speedy cheetah

What does this sound like? Zero to 90 kilometres per hour (55 mph) in just 3 seconds... a racing car perhaps? No, it's the top speed a cheetah can reach from a standing start.

It is by far the fastest land animal over a short distance, although its high-speed chases rarely last longer than 15 seconds over roughly 500 metres (1,640 ft). If a cheetah hasn't caught its prey within this time, it gives up... and the gazelle or antelope is free to run away!

Many centuries ago emperors, kings and noblemen would hunt antelope using trained cheetahs to track other animals.

Cheetah

THE WORLD'S BIGGEST CAT

Where do tigers live?

Tigers are found only in Asia. At the beginning of the 20th century around 100,000 tigers roamed freely in forests and jungles, swamps, grassland and mountain areas, but they were hunted relentlessly for sport and thousands were killed. Today there could be as few as 5,000 tigers left in the wild.

There are eight different species of tiger. Of these eight, three are thought to be extinct – the Balinese, the Javan and the Caspian tigers are gone forever.

The five species remaining are at risk – of the South China tiger, there are barely 80 left; the Sumatran number around 600; the small Indo-Chinese tiger, possibly 1,500; the big Siberian could number as few as 200. Of the Bengal tiger (which is the most common but still rare) there may be only 3,000 left in India, and fewer than a thousand in Bangladesh, Nepal and Bhutan all together.

However, many people, governments and wildlife organisations are working very hard to save the tiger and its home before it's too late!

How big is a tiger?

On average, a large male weighs about 200 kilograms (441 lb), a female around 150 kilograms (330 lb). The Siberian tiger, however, is much bigger, weighing up to 306 kilograms (675 lb) and measuring as long as 3.3 metres (10 ft 10 in) from head to tail. The farther north tigers live, the bigger they are.

Perfect camouflage

When a tiger is in long grass or walking in the dappled light of the forest, he seems to disappear because he is so well camouflaged. The pattern on his coat helps him to blend into the background perfectly.

Year of the tiger

The tiger is one of 12 animals in the Chinese calendar; the cycle means that each Chinese year is matched with an animal. The year 2000 will be the year of the dragon.

The white tiger

White tiger cubs are born into litters of cubs with normal colouring. These rare tigers are not a separate species but the result of a mutant gene. They are often born in captivity and can be seen in some zoos.

Do tigers like water?

Tigers love water and they are good swimmers. They often wade into pools and streams to escape the heat of the day.

These cats stay there for hours keeping cool, sometimes with just their head above water. But as they hate getting water in their eyes, tigers often enter a stream backwards!

When do tigers hunt?

Tigers usually hunt during the night from dusk to dawn, and they always hunt alone. They don't chase their prey across open spaces like a lion, instead they ambush or stalk it, crouching down on the ground and creeping slowly forward.

What do tigers eat?

They will eat whatever they can catch – mostly medium-sized prey such as deer, goats, wild pigs, and occasionally monkeys and peacocks.

A tiger will also kill larger animals such as cattle, water buffalo and sometimes even rhino and elephant calves. They drag their prey close to water as they need to drink often during their meal.

How much can tigers eat?

Tigers are the largest of all the big cats, so they need a lot to eat. They will devour 50-80 kilograms (110-176 lb) of meat in three to four days. Once a week, a tiger will kill an animal the size of a deer. Tigers are very capable hunters which means they seldom go hungry.

Babies with stripes

Just before her cubs are born, the tigress picks a safe place for her new family. She will have to choose carefully, because her cubs must be well hidden while she is away looking for food.

Usually the tigress hides them in thick grass, a cave or rocks, or perhaps in the hollow of a tree. Wild dogs and jackals often kill young cubs – so do male tigers sometimes!

A tigress may give birth to three or four cubs, occasionally as many as six. They are helpless at first, weighing about 1 kilogram (2.2 lb) and measuring about 46 centimetres (18 in) from nose to tail.

The cubs drink their mother's milk for about six months, but when they are about eight weeks old they begin to taste meat that their mother brings them.

If a tigress thinks that her cubs are in the slightest danger, she will move them to a safe home carrying them in her mouth one by one. By the time they are three months old tiger cubs are very playful. Already the tigress is teaching them to follow and keep close to her. She does this by quiet coughs, grunts and growls which the cubs soon learn to obey.

Cubs love to pounce on their mother's tail as she swishes it from side to side. They will jump on clumps of grass or anything that moves. They stalk birds like partridge and pheasant... this is how they learn to hunt.

Over the next 18 months the cubs will follow their mother learning how to fend for themselves, for soon it will be time for them to live on their own.

Where do lions and tigers live together?
In India, home of the tiger as well as the rare Asiatic lion. There are only some 300 of these maneless lions left in the wild.

Tiger indenticat!
You can tell one tiger from another as every single tiger has a different pattern of stripes on its face.

18

Fast food!

A tiger hunts using its eyes and ears rather than by smell. They prefer large animals, capturing them after a brief fast chase.

Tracking a tiger

Tigers mark their territory in special ways, letting everyone know that a certain area belongs to a particular tiger.

How can you tell if you are in tiger territory?

• Search the ground for pug marks (paw prints). These will tell you how big the tiger is, and if it is running or walking.

• Look at the tree trunks for long deep scratches made by the tiger's sharp claws. Remember to look up high – tigers are big!

• Use your nose! If a tiger has passed by, it will have left a scent behind. Another good clue is tiger droppings!

• Listen for the tiger's roar – it can be heard up to 3.2 kilometres (2 mi) away.

Footnote

During the 20th century, the tiger was hunted to near extinction. Its numbers have fallen by almost 95 per cent.

Much of the tiger's forest home has been cut down. Human populations have increased, which means less space for the tiger to roam.

In the last few years special laws have been passed to protect the tiger, and reserves have been set up for them to live and breed in safety.

Many countries have banned the trade of tiger skins for rugs, coats and trophies. Unfortunately poachers are still killing many tigers, for a high price is paid in some countries for tiger bones, which are ground up for use in some traditional Chinese medicines.

19

WHAT?
WHERE?
WHY?

Does anyone eat vultures?

Like Man, animals catch and eat all kinds of birds. The only bird that nobody makes a meal of is a vulture – they are inedible. Vulture casserole... not very appetising!

What is the main difference between a squid and an octopus?

A squid has ten tentacles – an octopus has eight.

What is the biggest animal that lives on land?

The elephant. The biggest sea animal is the blue whale.

What is the smallest mammal?

The bumblebee bat of Thailand, which really is as big as a bumblebee! Its body is 2.9 centimetres (1.1 in) long and weighs only 2 grams (0.07 ounces). The bumblebee bat was discovered only 25 years ago!

What is unusual about a dragonfly?

A dragonfly can fly forwards, backwards, hover, glide and stop in mid-air, but it cannot fold its wings! A dragonfly is a predatory insect and its diet consists mostly of smaller insects. They catch their food whilst in flight.

How did the hippopotamus get its name?

Hippos spend most of their day in rivers. Their name comes from the ancient Greek words for 'river' and 'horse'.

Which creature has the longest tongue?

The chameleon, whose tongue can measure up to one and a half times as long as its body! This crafty reptile shoots out its tongue to catch prey on the sticky tip, then reels it back in half a second!

How many ants does an anteater eat?

A giant anteater gobbles up over a million ants in one year... delicious!

Just how big is an ostrich egg?

This giant egg is equivalent to 24 hens' eggs. It measures 15-20 centimetres (6-8 in) long and 10-15 centimetres (4-6 in) in diameter.

It weighs up to 1.78 kilograms (3.9 lb)... now that really is the biggest egg!

Why do bees swarm?

Honey bees are social creatures – workers, drones and a queen all live together. Drones are the male bees whose only job is to mate with the queen! If a hive or nest becomes overcrowded, the old queen bee flies off with a swarm of bees to start a new colony, and a new queen will take over the old hive.

Is there such a thing as a timid alligator?

Believe it or not, there is! The rare Chinese alligator is quite small by alligator standards. An American alligator can reach 5.5 metres (18 ft) long, but the Chinese alligator grows to only 1.15 metres (4 ft).

It lives in the waters of the lower Yangtze river and feeds on frogs and fish... it's far too timid to go near humans.

In winter this alligator can remain in the frozen river, its body encased in ice with only its snout showing so it can breathe. They drop their body temperature and stay there until the spring warmth melts the ice.

Light as a feather!

Did you know that the weight of the feathers of some birds is greater than the weight of all their bones?

How BIG?

Once the biggest reptile that walked the Earth, this now extinct dinosaur is known as the 'Earth-shaker'... I expect you can guess why!

The seismosaurus weighed an estimated 80 tons and was a staggering 37 metres (120 ft) long, and lived during the late Jurassic period. This is about the same length as a blue whale, yet amazingly, the 'Earth-shaking' dinosaur weighed only half as much. Its skeleton was found in new Mexico, USA, about 15 years ago.

Do birds have teeth?

No, their food is swallowed whole. It passes to their gizzard where it is ground up by the muscles in the walls.

Swans, geese and flamingos have fine, sharp, comb-like teeth on the edges of their bills. These teeth sieve particles of food from the water. Geese use them when they are grazing. The teeth can also give you a nasty nip if you argue with a gander!

Why do elephants flap their ears?

When elephants need to keep cool on very hot days, they flap their ears, which helps them to lower their body temperature.

African elephants have bigger ears than their Indian cousins. Elephants' huge ears can be up to 1.5 metres (5 ft) long. They act as ready-made fans – the hotter the sun, the faster they flap!

What is a flying fox?

A flying fox is a bat, and not a fox at all! Some fruitbats are called flying foxes because their heads look more like a fox than a bat.

Take care not to stand under a tree where flying foxes are roosting. These bats eat blossoms and some fruit which they crush between their jaws, then they swallow the juice and spit out the pulp which drops on anyone standing below!

Why do camels have big feet?

If camels had small sharp hooves like horses, they would surely sink into the soft desert sand!

Having big feet enables the camel to spread its weight over a larger area, so they can travel across the sand with ease. This is why the camel is known as the 'ship of the desert'. They also have padded toes so that they can walk on the hot desert sand.

Which bird sunbathes?

The cormorant is an aquatic bird which lives on the fish it catches underwater. But the cormorant doesn't have a gland that produces oil to make its feathers waterproof – as most other water birds do.

So after every dive, the cormorant has to spread his wings and 'sunbathe' so his feathers can dry in the sun.

What can turn the sea a different colour?

Plankton! Sometimes there are so many of these minute creatures drifting near the surface of the water, the sea turns green and sometimes red. A blue whale eats up to four tons of plankton a day!

Whose egg is only as big as a pea?

There is a hummingbird that lives in Jamaica whose tiny egg is only 10 millimetres (0.39 in) in length and weighs just 0.365 grams (0.0128 oz).

The egg is not quite as big as a pea, and is the smallest egg on record!

How do earthworms dig?

A worm's body must always be kept damp. If it is exposed to the sun or hot air, it will dry up and die very quickly.

Worms dig into the soil by using their muscles. As the earthworm burrows head-first through the damp earth, it swallows some of the soil.

The worm extracts vegetable matter from the soil as food, then it expels the soil in the shape of a wormcast which you see all over your lawn.

Where will you find unicorns and centaurs?

You will only find these creatures in books! A unicorn, from Western and Eastern mythology, is like a horse but has a horn growing out of its forehead. A centaur, from Greek mythology, is half man and half horse – it is a man from head to waist.

THOSE ENORMOUS ELEPHANTS

Elephants are the largest animals that live on land. An African male elephant can weigh as much as six or even seven cars – that's over six tons! They can stand as high as 3.7 metres (12 ft), with the bull (male), slightly bigger than the female (called a cow).

Huge animals have huge appetites! An adult elephant will eat 170 kilograms (375 lb) of plant food a day, and needs to drink 90 litres (20 gallons) of water... that's about 12 buckets full!

African and Asian

There are two types of elephant: the African and the Asian. The African elephant is the larger of the pair. Unfortunately, they live so far apart, these cousins never meet! African elephants inhabit forests, grasslands, and deserts while Asian elephants live in tropical grassy plains and rainforests.

Both species are endangered. The African elephant is under threat from poachers hunting for ivory, and the Asian elephant's living space is getting smaller as human populations increase.

What's the difference?

African elephants have huge flapping ears shaped like Africa on the map. Asian elephants' ears are much smaller, and the bottom part looks just like a map of India!

The Asian elephant has very short or no tusks at all, a smooth trunk, a high curved back, a bumpy forehead, and one finger-like shape on the tip of its trunk.

The African elephant has long tusks, a ridged trunk, a dip in its back, round forehead, and the tip of its trunk has two finger-like shapes.

One big family

Groups of elephant families stay together to form a herd, often up to a hundred animals. The groups consist of adult females (some with babies), aunties and cousins, who all help to look after each other.

Elephants meet and greet one another by touching the other's mouth with the tip of its trunk.

Young males leave the family at around age 15, to join the other bulls or go off on their own. Young females stay with the family for life.

Jumbo on the job

Sadly, many Asian elephants are trained and forced to work. They can understand up to 30 words of command, and often lift heavy logs up to two tons.

Most working elephants are born in captivity. Sometimes they take part in religious processions, splendidly dressed and decorated.

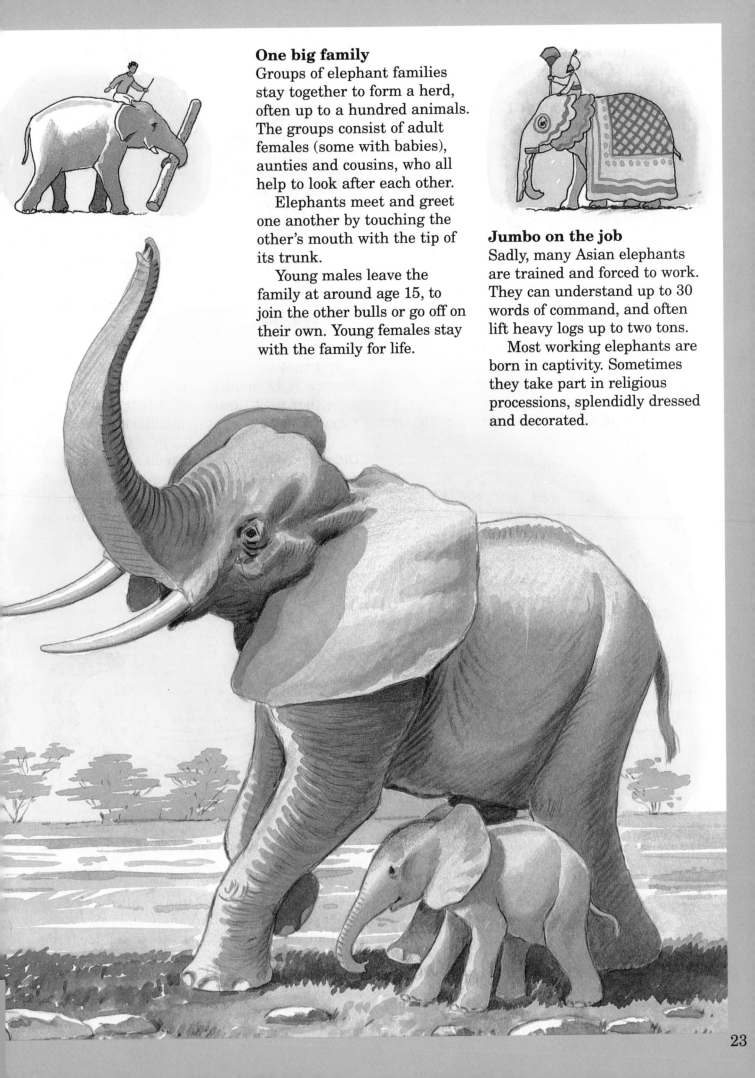

Elephant trunks...

An elephant's trunk is a long nose ending with a top lip at the end – rather like a long arm with a hand at the bottom. Elephants use their trunks in many ways.

As an elephant can't reach the ground with its mouth or tongue, it has to use its trunk to pick up food. Trunks can reach high up into trees to gather leaves or break off branches.

When an elephant is in danger, it raises its trunk up high, flaps its ears out to the side, then charges at 40 kilometres per hour (25 mph).

...and tusks

Are you right-handed or left-handed? Elephants are either right-tusked or left-tusked, and the majority use the right – just like humans!

Did you know that an elephant's massive tusks are front teeth? Imagine what that would feel like! They continue to grow all through an elephant's life. One of the largest tusks ever measured was 3.5 metres (11 ft 6 in) long.

When an elephant crosses a river or dips underwater when bathing, it uses its trunk as a snorkel! Trunks are powerful enough to lift up a tree, and so sensitive they can pick up a tiny berry.

Elephants can dig deeply with their tusks when they are searching for water or salts.

Tusks are made of a substance called ivory. Cruel poachers kill many thousands of elephants and take their tusks to sell for large amounts of money. The ivory is carved into intricate ornaments and sold again. Not every country has barred the trade in ivory, but the countries of North America and Europe have.

The elephant drinks by sucking up water through its trunk, then squirting it into its mouth. It can also use its trunk as a shower, to cool off on hot days.

Can you see a likeness?

Every animal we know of today has evolved over millions of years, in many kinds of different ways. More than 50 million years ago, the elephant, the manatee and the hyrax all came from the same family. Although they look very different, they are closely related.

An ancient jumbo!

One ancestor of the elephant, the woolly mammoth, was roaming the Earth at the same time as cavemen. Compare the two pictures below. Not a lot of difference is there?

The hyrax

Amazingly, this furry little animal from Africa, weighing at the most 5.4 kilograms (12 lb), is related to the jumbo! Its dainty little feet are remarkably similar to those of the elephant.

The manatee

This large, slow-moving, docile creature lives in shallow tropical waters and rivers.

The manatee doesn't have to be told to "eat up its greens" as it chomps through a massive 75 kilograms (165 lb) of sea grass and water plants every day! Don't you think that its head looks a bit like an elephant's?

Baby elephant facts

A female elephant has her first baby when she is 12-15 years old.

Elephants have the longest gestation period (pregnancy) of any mammal – 22 months.

Newborns drink Mum's milk with their mouth, not with their trunk.

A baby has milk teeth known as 'tushes'. After a few months it learns to eat plants, but still has milk teeth until it is two years old. As an adult, it will eat 170 kilograms (375 lb) of plant material a day.

An elephant calf is a really big baby! At birth it may measure about 1 metre (3 ft) tall and weigh 120 kilograms (265 lb).

A baby elephant is quite hairy when first born. Although rather wobbly on its legs, the little calf can walk after a few hours and keep up with the herd within a couple of days.

It takes the calf about six months to learn how to use its trunk.

Elephants' tusks first appear at age two.

By the time a young elephant is six years old it will weigh 1,000 kilograms (2,200 lb).

Elephants stop growing at about age 15.

An elephant can live for 60 years in the wild and up to 80 years in captivity.

ANIMAL ALLSORTS

It's a long walk round!

The caribou of Canada and Alaska, when they migrate, make the longest journey of any land animal.

Tens of thousands of animals gather in huge herds and move along the same routes. They travel north to the Arctic tundra where their young are born. Then they graze all summer, particularly on 'reindeer moss'.

When they return south along the same route, they will have travelled an incredible 2,250 kilometres (1,400 mi).

Enormous pipelines that carry oil and gas from Arctic reserves lay across some of their routes. In this frozen wilderness, the pipelines have to be laid above the rock-hard ground – right in the path of the caribou.

To combat this problem the engineers have raised the pipes up on a bridge high enough for the caribou to pass underneath.

Bottoms up!

The darkling beetle in Africa's Namib desert is up before dawn. He climbs to the top of a sand dune and does a handstand, tilting his body forward.

As moist air blows in from the Atlantic, condensation forms on the beetle's shiny back and rolls down the ridges and into his mouth... what a refreshing drink!

The bird that never gets stung

The bee-eater seizes bees and wasps with its slender beak as they fly past. It will hammer the insect on a branch, look carefully to find out which end of the wasp or bee contains the sting, which it rubs off onto the branches. The bee-eater then gobbles up the insect. Colonies of rainbow-coloured bee-eaters dig out tunnels in steep river banks. These tunnels open up into underground chambers which contain nests where they rear their young.

Parasol parade!

In fine dry weather, leaf-cutting ants are busy all day cutting up pieces of leaves and flowers, then carrying them back to their underground nest. You can see them marching along in a trail, looking like a parade of parasols.

Inside the nest are compost gardens made of chewed up leaves and saliva. The gardens grow a fungus on which the ants feed.

These busy ants never collect leaves when it's raining. Only dry leaves are needed in the chambers of the ant colony... perhaps they've never thought of using the leaves as umbrellas!

THE GRACEFUL GIANT

The giraffe is by far the world's tallest animal. It can grow to a height of 6.1 metres (20 ft) which is about the same as a two-storey house! These gigantic animals can weigh over 1,600 kilograms (3,525 lb).

A prickly meal

The giraffe feeds on treetop vegetation that is far beyond the reach of other browsing animals. Even the thorns of the spiky acacia bushes (which are sharp enough to puncture car tyres) make a tasty meal for a giraffe!

You can tell the sex of a giraffe from a distance by the way it feeds. The male stretches out his neck and head as far as he can reach, the female bends her neck over to feed on the leaves at a lower level.

Long tall babies

A newborn giraffe calf stands as high as a tall man. This big baby is 1.8 metres (6.2 ft) tall and weighs a hefty 102 kilograms (224 lb). Young giraffes can double their weight in less than two years.

How does a giraffe drink?

Giraffes find it difficult to bend their long legs or kneel, so they splay out their front legs, bend their knees a little and lower their long necks to drink.

It's a knockout!

When a giraffe is standing upright feeding, then bends down to drink, it lowers its head 2 metres (6.4 ft). But the giraffe's huge heart, weighing 12 kilograms (26.5 lb) together with unique valves and stretchy blood vessels in its 2.5 metre (8.2 ft) neck, keep the blood supply to its head flowing at a constant pressure... otherwise the giraffe would become unconscious.

Long-necked wrestlers

Young bulls (male giraffes) intertwine their long necks – rather like crossing your fingers. They push each other from side to side, they're not really fighting – just testing one another!

The giraffe's finger print

Giraffes don't have fingers but their marking or patterns act like a human finger print. No two giraffes are alike. Every animal has its own distinctive pattern on its coat; from birth to death they remain the same!

Did you know?

• There are nine different kinds of giraffe living in Africa.
• One powerful kick from the front feet of a giraffe can kill a lion.
• Giraffes 'ruminate' or 'chew the cud', just like cows!

The unknown animal

Most of the world knew nothing about the okapi until 1900. This shy timid animal is the giraffe's closest relative. It lives in remote forest in northern Zaire, but is rarely seen. The head of the okapi resembles the giraffe, but its body is more like a zebra's, with stripes on its hind quarters. Both okapis and giraffes have tongues measuring up to half a metre long!

THAT'S REVOLTING!
(not to be read before meals!)

• What's worse than finding a caterpillar in your apple? Finding half of one!

• Some surgeons still use blood-sucking leeches in tricky operations to maintain circulation in small blood vessels.

• The gulper eel has such a flexible stomach that it can swallow fish which are bigger than its own body!

• A penguin's tongue is covered in minute spines – perfect for gripping slippery slimy fish!

• In very hot climates lizards must always have water in their bodies, so their urine is sometimes a sloppy paste.

• Crickets make a meal of other insects, and sometimes even their own young!

• The codling moth lays its eggs on fruit trees. When the caterpillars hatch, they crawl inside the fruit and stay there, slowly munching until they turn into a pupa… so be careful when you bite into your apple!

• If you put ten elephants in your garden for a day, you will end up with one ton of dung to put round your roses!

• The silvery slimy trail that a snail leaves behind protects its foot from scratches.

• The female lyrebird carries worms and grubs inside special pouches in her cheeks to feed her chicks. Then she stores her chicks' droppings in her empty cheeks to bury later in the day.

• Housefly maggots love to dine on dung and left-over food, especially if it's rotten.

• No wonder goats can be smelly! As well as using their anal scent glands, they often spray themselves with urine.

• Vultures have very few feathers on their heads and necks. This stops them from getting messy at mealtimes when they stick their heads inside gory carcasses.

• After a shower of rain, paper wasps like to spit! To stop their paper nests from disintegrating when wet, they lap up the water and spit it out.

• If a crab tries to eat a slime star starfish, it will be in for a shock. This starfish instantly secretes a thick slimy mucus all over its enemies… and it's poisonous too!

• When male African hunting dogs return from a hunting trip, they can't wait to be sick! They are simply regurgitating lumps of meat from the animals they have killed, to feed the female and her cubs.

• A kingfisher's nest is a real tip! The floor is littered with stinking scraps of old fish and bits of insects. These smelly remains attract swarms of tiny flies which feed on them.

• If you spot a heron's nest high up in the trees and you stand underneath it, keep very still! When heron chicks are disturbed, they stick their beaks over the rim of the nest and drop globs of half-digested fish onto anything below.

• Cockroaches chew up the food left lying around in your house, leaving a dreadful stench as they drop oily secretions everywhere.

• In one way baby kingfishers do their bit to tidy the nest. They poke their rear ends through the nest hole and shoot out their droppings!

• Believe it or not, there is an animal that can give off a far worse stink than a skunk. The African gorilla can swing its hindquarters in front of an enemy and spray out the foulest-smelling liquid in nature!

• There is a parrot that thinks it's a vulture! The kea from New Zealand loves feeding on the carcasses of dead sheep. Pretty polly? We don't think so!

• The butcherbird skewers any food it can't eat on thorns and sometimes barbed wire. Larger prey is jammed onto a fork of two branches – its easier to deal with that way.

• The spitting spider prowls by night. When it spots a likely meal, it moves in close and squirts a jet of gum. This forms a net of sticky threads that tie up the victim.

• The human head louse has special claws to hang on to your hair while it feeds on the dead skin of your scalp.

• The spitting cobra from Mozambique can hit its target every time, even when it's 3 metres (10 ft) away.

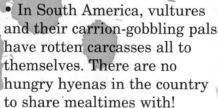

• In South America, vultures and their carrion-gobbling pals have rotten carcasses all to themselves. There are no hungry hyenas in the country to share mealtimes with!

• Rabbits and hares often eat their droppings. Dry droppings are left, but soft droppings are eaten and passed through their system once more, as they contain valuable nutrients.

• Dominant male rhinos and hippos mark their territory with gigantic piles of dung which they scatter in all directions.

• If you annoy a camel, it will certainly spit at you. But did you know that camels spit out their stinking liquid from their stomachs?!

• Vampire bats drink the blood of cattle. They prefer to stick to the same breed of cattle all their lives.

• When a leech wants to suck your blood, it makes a small cut with its sharp-toothed jaw. But don't worry, you won't feel a thing – anaesthetic in the leech's saliva numbs the wound.

• People eat the strangest things in different parts of the world: fat caterpillars, juicy grubs, crunchy ants and grasshoppers. But would you have the appetite for a tarantula spider as big as a dinner plate? Some tribes in the Amazon rainforest consider it a treat. They take off the legs then barbecue the rest… delicious!

• What makes a bird feel sick and retch? The monarch butterfly, because it tastes so foul and it's poisonous.

• As well as smelling revolting, the spray from a skunk can even cause temporary blindness if aimed at the face.

• Nightjars rest on the ground during the day. As soon as darkness falls, off they fly hoping to catch lots of airborne insects in their very wide mouths. Now nightjars love moths, and moths can't resist flying near lights, so any camp site with lanterns and lamps is like a 'fly-in' diner to a nightjar!

• When a stink snake raises its head, run away as fast as you can! It's about to release a terrible smell like rotten eggs, which lasts for hours.

• Always check your apples! The female apple maggot lays her eggs under the skin of overripe fruit. The maggots then mature into flies.

• Wolverines bite bears on the bottom! These vicious animals, as big as a medium-size dog, have such powerful jaws they will tackle anything, from moose and caribou to pumas, wolves and bears.

• The eggs of the dragonfly hatch into tiny nymphs that live underwater – they look like small brown dragonflies, but without any wings. When they need to escape from their enemies, the nymphs squirt water out of their bottoms so quickly that it propels them out of danger's way!

• When the stinkpot turtle releases its nasty smell, any creature that has already captured the turtle will drop it immediately, as the smell is so awful!

• There is a leech that feeds only on hippos' blood – it's called the hippopotamus leech. Birds that perch on hippos often pick off these leeches and gobble them up along with other parasites.

• Many lizards are able to shed their tail when grabbed at the rear by an enemy, but the skink goes one step further. It sheds its tail, runs off, then scampers back to eat it!

• The larvae of the dor beetle feed on cow dung. Yuck! The adult beetle digs tunnels under cowpats in which to house its larvae, and so the larvae grow up in a home filled with dung!

• The female digger wasp catches a spider, paralyses it with her sting, drags it back to her burrow, lays an egg on it and then seals the burrow. The spider provides quite enough food to live on until the larva becomes an adult wasp months later.

• With some species of the praying mantis, the female eats the male alive while mating. She will bite off his head, then crunch and munch away until her mate has vanished!

• If you were a housefly, this would be your favourite menu… fresh horse dung, pig and human excrement. Then you might visit someone's dinner table, settle on their meal and proceed to vomit all over it! But that's not all – these pests also carry over six million bacteria on their feet at a time. No wonder so many people detest these pests!

• The South American hoatzin (or the 'stinkbird') is considered the world's smelliest bird! It smells of rotting compost or cow manure… due to lots of green leaves fermenting in its digestive system… nice!

• Do you like garlic? If you dig around in a compost heap, you might find some garlic glass snails, which smell very strongly of garlic!

• Mosquitoes suck the blood of animals as well as humans. In summer, a caribou in Alaska can lose up to 1.1 litres (2 pints) of blood in a week.

• Caterpillars eat so much and grow so quickly that their skin repeatedly splits and falls off.

• In autumn moles store tasty earthworms (after biting off the heads) inside their underground 'larder'.

THE RARE RHINO

There were many types of rhino roaming the Earth 40 million years ago. Some were no bigger than a dog, others had long legs like a horse. The giant hornless rhinoceros, the baluchitherium, is said to be the largest land mammal that ever lived. It stood almost 5.5 metres (18 ft) at the shoulder, and its skull measured about 1.2 metres (4 ft).

Two million years ago some of the ancestors of the animals we know today, such as elk and deer, were gigantic. The woolly rhinos even had horns over 1.8 metres (6 ft) long, and they were around until about 15,000 years ago!

Over all those years different species of rhino were plentiful. Sadly, the five remaining species on Earth today are all threatened with extinction. The danger comes from poachers who kill the rhino just for its horn. Ground up into powder, the horn is used in the Far East in some traditional medicines. In the Middle East, the horn is in demand for the making of dagger handles, which are considered a symbol of great wealth.

Rhinoceroses are mammals which belong to the perissodactyla order along with horses and tapirs (an animal which looks like a pig, but is more closely related to rhinos). Rhinos are herbivores – meaning that they eat plant material, as opposed to hunting other animals. Animals which hunt other animals for food are known as carnivores, although they may eat plant material too.

How do you tell the white rhino from the black rhino?

Both of these rhinos live in Africa and they are similar in colour. They are both grey, not black or white! Each species has two horns, but the shape of their mouths is very different.

The white rhino has a wide square lip, like a cow, for cropping the grass it grazes on. The male is quite a heavyweight, weighing up to 3.5 tons!

The smaller black rhino has a pointed mouth for browsing on shrubs and biting off leaves; it weighs up to 1.5 tons. These huge animals can live for up to 45 years.

Black rhino

• Oxpecker birds and cattle egrets are the rhino's constant companions. They pick and gobble up the ticks and parasites that lodge in the creases of the rhino's leathery skin.

• The Greek word 'rhinoceros' means 'horn-nose'. A rhino's horn is not made of bone attached to the skull – it is a big solid mass of hair fibres that has grown from the skin on top of the nose.

• Some species of rhino can be extremely aggressive and often charge at people without warning. They can ram and overturn vehicles when provoked.

Out of Africa!

The two-ton Indian rhino you see here looks as if it is wearing armour-plating. It never uses its single horn for fighting… it bites instead!

The Sumatran rhino is the smallest of the rhinos, measuring little more than a metre high. It has patches of long hair on its neck, back and legs – but not as much as its ancestor, the woolly rhino, had millions of years ago!

The Javan rhino could be the rarest large animal left in the world today… there are only about 50 of them.

Indian rhino

White rhino

BELIEVE IT OR NOT

New 'gnashers'

Crocodiles swallow some of their meals whole, but they have to pull apart large prey. In doing so, quite often they will lose several teeth. Luckily they can grow new ones quickly. So crocodiles may have around 50 sets of new gnashers during their lifetime!

Does a mouse make you shriek?

Well the mighty wetapunga would! This gigantic cricket from New Zealand is as big as a mouse and weighs five times as much, 70 grams (2.5 oz). It cannot fly or jump too high… what a relief!

Lazy lunch

The echidna's nostrils and mouth are at the very tip of his long snout. On days when this spiky little anteater is feeling lazy, he will stretch out on a termite mound and stick out his saliva-coated tongue. When the tongue is covered with tasty insects, the echidna gobbles them up with no effort at all.

Pigs go for a paddle

A few years ago wild pigs on a South Pacific island went paddling in the shallow reef around the island, in search of food. They dipped their snouts into the water and began to sample the seafood. The pigs found that they really enjoyed it, and eagerly gobbled up mussels, oysters and even slimy sea slugs!

Not for sale!

The barn owl roosts in hollow trees and very often in old buildings and ruins. Church towers and farmers' barns are home to the most widespread of the world's owls. The female doesn't build a proper nest, but lays her eggs on old feathers, dirt, dust and cobwebs that have collected over the years. But this is just what barn owls love; they are happy in the same home for most of their lives.

Can an insect make pots?

The female potter wasp makes several 'pots' from wet clay. After the pots have dried, she will choose one of them and fill it with caterpillars. Then she will lay her egg inside her pot. Once the egg hatches, the larva has plenty of food to eat until it changes into a pupa. When the new wasp comes out of its cocoon, it breaks open the clay pot and flies away.

When gorillas go grey

A gorilla with grey fur is a mature male, not an old gorilla whose fur is turning white with age. Mature males are known as 'silverbacks' because of the broad band of grey hair across their backs.

Role reversal

Sea horses are unusual creatures – it is the male who gives birth. The female sea horse deposits eggs in the male's pouch, and the eggs hatch after about 10 days.

Red for danger

The vibrant colouring of the poison-dart frog warns its enemies to beware! Lizards, birds and snakes all give this tiny bright red frog a miss, as the poison from the skin glands on its back is deadly!

Do snakes eat their greens?

Definitely not! Snakes are not vegetarians. They only eat meat, often in the form of mice, rats, frogs, lizards and all kinds of creepy-crawlies… so nobody ever makes a snake eat up his Brussels sprouts!

Winning by a nose!

The male proboscis monkey from Borneo must take the prize for the largest, longest and oddest-shaped nose of all. The female has a small snub nose and, more often than not, she chooses the male with the biggest nose for a mate… so the male proboscis monkey really does win by a nose!

SSSSPECTACULAR SNAKES

Snakes that kill their prey by crushing or squeezing, then swallowing it whole, are called constrictors. This group contains some of the largest snakes in the world: the anacondas, the boa constrictors and the pythons. The biggest of them all, the South American anaconda, may grow over 11 metres (36 ft) long.

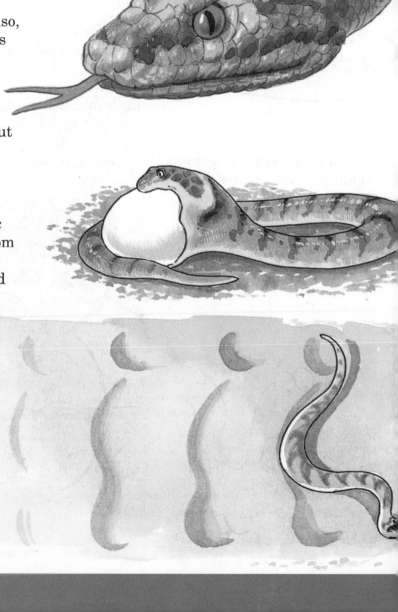

Can snakes fly?
The flying snake from Southeast Asia doesn't actually fly – it glides! These snakes coil up, then launch themselves from one tree to another. They can spread their ribs to flatten and widen their bodies, often steering from side to side through the branches.

How does a snake crack an egg?
The African egg-eating snake can swallow an egg twice the size of its head. A bony hinge which connects its jaw unhooks when something huge is about to be swallowed. Also, the snake's bottom jaw consists of two halves joined by a stretchy elastic ligament, so the snake can open its mouth really wide!
A pointed bone in the back of the snake's throat pierces a hole in the eggshell. Then the snake swallows the contents and spits out the bits of shell.

Why do some snakes move sideways?
Snakes that live in sandy deserts move in a special way. They form a loop or raised arc with their bodies, then throw themselves from side to side… it's called 'sidewinding'. Some snakes must move like this because the sand has no grip; it also stops the underneath of their bodies from burning on the hot sand.

How can you tell if a cobra is cross?
An angry cobra raises its head and spreads out flaps of skin on its neck to form a hood. This cobra is cross and about to attack!

Did you know?

• The spectacled cobra has a pattern on the back of its hood that looks like a pair of spectacles.

• The African spitting cobra can spit poison towards the face and eyes from a distance of 2 metres (6.6 ft)!

• Not all snakes are as big as the South American anaconda; the Texas slender blind snake can measure as little as 13 centimetres (5 inches) in length.

What makes a rattlesnake rattle?

Bony scales on the end of a rattlesnake's tail make a noise like a baby's rattle when the snake feels threatened… the whirring sound is simply a warning! Every time a rattlesnake sheds its skin, a scale is left behind at the tip of the tail. The rattle is a build-up of scales that fit loosely together time after time when the skin is shed.

Fooled you!

Some snakes have skins with bright colours and strong patterns. This warns enemies to keep well away – usually they are deadly poisonous! Snakes that are quite harmless often have similar patterns and colouring. It's a wonderful disguise – enemies always leave them alone!

ANIMAL ALLSORTS

Are bats the only mammals that can fly?
Other mammals, like flying squirrels and lemurs, are leaping or gliding and not really flying at all. The bat is the only mammal that can fly.

Line-dancing lobsters
In autumn, when thousands of spiny lobsters migrate from shallow reefs to deep water for breeding, they travel across the open sea bed in long lines, covering distances of up to 150 kilometres (93 mi). Each lobster hooks its front legs around the tail of the one in front, then off they go. If you were swimming alongside, you couldn't keep up with them, they move faster than you!

Counting sheep
Sheep use more than half the land in Australia for grazing… that's not surprising, as there are 137 million of them! Australian sheep are mostly merinos. This breed of sheep produces lots of fine wool… almost three quarters of the woollen clothing of the world is made from the fleeces of all those Australian sheep!

Why does a dog 'prick up' its ears?
Dogs have excellent hearing. They 'prick up' or move their ears to find out exactly where the sound is coming from.

Which bird lives the longest?
The sulphur crested cockatoo. One of these birds died at London Zoo when it was over 80 years old. Cockatoos are only found in the Australasian regions. They are not as brightly coloured as parrots, they are mainly plain – black or white. The cockatoo's feathers have a different structure which does not produce the reds, greens, blues and yellows of a parrot's plumage.

Can you follow an elephant's trail?
You might find it difficult if you are looking for huge, deep footprints! The heaviest animal that walks on Earth has big feet which cover a large area. So the elephant's weight is spread, leaving very few marks on damp ground, and hardly any on a dry track.

Blind as a bat!
Baby bats are born blind, but after a while their eyes open – just like a kitten! Grown bats are not blind at all. They can see perfectly well in daylight, but not too well at night when they are hunting. Bats locate their prey by sending out high-pitched squeaks. The sound bounces off any object in its path and the bat's ears pick up the echo, then the bat can find the prey.

Ask Santa!
There's a certain way that reindeer are different from all other species of deer… Santa knows the answer!

Reindeer are the only deer that pull loads. An adult reindeer can easily trot across the snow pulling a lightweight sled, carrying the weight of three adults, for up to 40 kilometres (25 mi) a day. However, we are told that they travel much faster and farther through the sky on Christmas Eve!

A brand new baby!

A brand new breed has just hit the headlines. Rama, a soft woolly 'cama', was born in 1998. Vets had crossed a female llama and a male camel – and Rama was created!

Why are dolphins and whales born tail first?

As a rule, babies are born head first and begin to breathe immediately. Baby whales and dolphins are born underwater, tail first, to prevent them from drowning. They must reach the surface of the ocean as quickly as possible to take their first breath of air and fill their lungs.

The newborn calves, who can swim straightaway, are helped to the surface by their mothers and 'aunts'. These are other female whales or dolphins who live together in small groups. Often a group of killer whales will stay together for life!

Which zebra has the most stripes?

The Grevys zebra, from northern East Africa, has more stripes than other species – as their markings are narrower, there are more of them. Not so long ago Grevys zebras were hunted for skins to make handbags. Now, luckily, they are protected.

Off to see the world!

For a baby hedgehog, life with Mum is short and sweet. When they are born, hedgehog babies have around a hundred soft white spines. The stiff brown ones start appearing in about a week, and at just eleven days old they can roll up into a ball, like Mum!

When the little hedgehogs are a month old, and by now covered in prickles, their mother takes them out to forage for food. They love beetles, caterpillars and slugs, in fact, all creepy-crawlies at ground level are tasty treats for young hedgehogs. After another ten days or so, when the little hedgehogs are nearly six weeks old, off they go into the wide world... perhaps one is heading for your garden!

Who can eat a boat for lunch?

It's not a huge creature as you may imagine, but a really tiny one! Shipworms munch their way through wooden boats and piers and pilings. This small mollusc bores into wood with its sharp shell-covered head. It moves along gobbling up wet wood for every meal. It's known as the 'termite of the sea'. Shipworms were the reason Christopher Columbus was left stranded in Jamaica for a year! He eventually reached Spain in 1504.

Is it a moth or a butterfly?

Moths are closely related to butterflies – both are from the second largest insect order, lepidoptera. Butterflies fly by day, moths by night.

Butterflies rest with their wings folded upright while moths hold them out flat over their bodies.

Have you tried this tongue twister?

'How much wood would a woodchuck chuck If a woodchuck could chuck wood?'

We don't think he would 'chuck' a great deal, as he spends as much as eight months of the year fast asleep! The woodchuck, or groundhog, so the story goes, is supposed to wake up on the 2nd of February each year – this is know to Americans as 'Groundhog Day'.

During the lengthy time the woodchuck is hibernating in its burrow, his body temperature drops to just a few degrees above freezing point, and when he wakes up in spring, the woodchuck has lost half his body weight. Late summer is spent eating as much food as possible to convert to fat for the next eight months' sleep.

How soon can ducklings swim?

Almost as soon as they hatch! The duckling's feathers take an hour or two to dry when it comes out of its egg. Then it follows its mother to the nearest water, jumps in and starts swimming at once.

MONKEYS AND APES

Of all the animals living on Earth today, monkeys and apes are most like Man, and our early ancestors would certainly have been ape-like creatures. Like us, monkeys and apes are social mammals, living in families or groups and bringing up their young together. On this page are some of the primates known as the lesser apes – the greater apes are gorillas, chimpanzees and orang-utans.

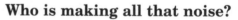

Howler monkey

Male mandrill

Who is making all that noise?

Howler monkeys of Central and South America make such a loud noise they can be heard up to 5 kilometres (3 mi) away.

A special shaped chamber in their throats makes their barks and howls seem even louder. At dawn and nightfall, the forest is filled with the noisy calls of howler monkeys.

Which monkey has a blue and red face?

The male mandrill that lives in the rainforests of West Africa has a startling red and blue face; the colours become much brighter when he is angry!

These baboons live in family groups of 15-20, some with babies riding on their backs. They spend the day on the ground searching for insects and fruit, but sleep up in the trees.

Baboons are the largest of the monkeys. They have long sabre-like teeth and a muzzle similar to a dog. These animals can be very aggressive and a group of them will sometimes attack and kill a leopard!

The acrobatic ape

Gibbons are the most agile of all the primates. They are amazing acrobats with a wonderful sense of balance. These small apes can run along branches steadying themselves with their long arms as if they were on a tightrope! They can walk on their hind legs and, with their powerful elongated arms, can swing hand over hand through the trees with ease. Baby gibbons cling on tightly to the front of their mothers as they leap and swing through the branches.

Gibbon

Monkeys in the moonlight

The night, or owl, monkey looks like an owl – it even hoots like one! These South American rainforest monkeys only come out to feed after sunset. They can see perfectly in the dark to hunt frogs, lizards and insects, and pick fruit and leaves. The males only call or hoot to females on very bright moonlit nights!

Special tails

Most South American monkeys have a prehensile tail, a special tail that can grip things – just like a fifth limb! This tail can support the whole weight of the monkey, leaving it free to feed, especially on food that would otherwise be out of reach. It also anchors the monkeys safely to branches.

43

The old man of the woods

The orang-utan's name is Malaysian for 'the old man of the woods'. These orange-haired apes are found only in the jungles of Borneo and Sumatra. Their arms are very strong, and their hands and feet are hook-shaped, as most of their time is spent climbing and swinging from branch to branch. An orang-utan's legs are not designed for walking as they rarely visit the ground, except to collect broken branches to build their nests for the night.

Giants of the forest

Gorillas were once thought of as violent and dangerous animals, but studies in the wild have found them to be peaceful and gentle creatures. They spend their day in groups of around ten; the leader is an adult male, the rest are females with their babies. They roam the forest all day, quietly feeding on leaves and branches or resting for a few hours at a time. When gorilla groups cross paths, it is rare that fighting occurs. Powerful displays of chest-beating serve to reduce tensions and avoid actual bloodshed.

A bed for the night

Every single night, gorillas build flat platforms with twigs and branches in the lower parts of trees. These are their beds for the night, but the heavy adult males make their leafy beds on the ground. Only young gorillas spend lots of time climbing and swinging through the trees... most of the adults are too heavy!

The biggest ape of all

Gorillas are the largest of the primates (mammals that include apes, monkeys and humans). Along with the chimpanzee, the gorilla is Man's closest relative. Adult male gorillas weigh up to 180 kilograms (400 lb), and stand up to 1.8 metres (6 ft) tall. They are stocky and solidly built with huge neck and shoulder muscles... their chest measurement is twice the size of a man's, and their armspan is long enough to go round three adults!

The mighty gorilla

Not a bit like King Kong!

When a male gorilla senses danger, he dashes from side to side, roaring loudly and beating his chest. This is to let his family group know where he is and to tell them to keep close by for protection. Displays of chest thumping are a show of strength and are used to frighten off rival males, as gorillas rarely fight with one another.

Newborn gorillas are quite small, just over 1.8 kilograms (4 lb), which is less than a human newborn baby. They are fed by their mother until they are three years old. A gorilla can live to the age of 40.

The clever chimpanzee

Chimps have large brains and are very intelligent. Some of their behaviour is similar to that of humans. In the wild they have learned to use simple tools, usually to obtain food. Chimps know how to use heavy rocks and sticks to crack the hard shells of nuts and fruit. They make sponges of chewed bark or leaves to collect drinking water.

If they want a quick meal of termites, chimps poke a thick stick into the mound, wait patiently for the ants to crawl up, then pull out the stick and lick them all off!

Although the chimp's diet is mainly vegetarian, they also eat insects, eggs and small birds. Male chimps sometimes go hunting in packs, and kill small pigs and deer and ambush other monkeys.

There are two species of chimpanzee living in tropical Africa. The common chimpanzee lives both in forests and open grassland, and the pygmy chimpanzee (which is not much different in size) lives only in tropical forests. Male chimps weigh about 40 kilograms (88 lb) and are just under a metre tall. They are much heavier in captivity.

Chimpanzees live in groups numbering up to 150 animals. Mothers spend most of their time grooming and playing with their young. A baby chimp clings to its mother's tummy until it is six months old, then it climbs up onto her back. Male chimps in the group often challenge one another, becoming aggressive, fighting, screaming, biting and even throwing sticks and stones at each other!

FASCINATING FACTS

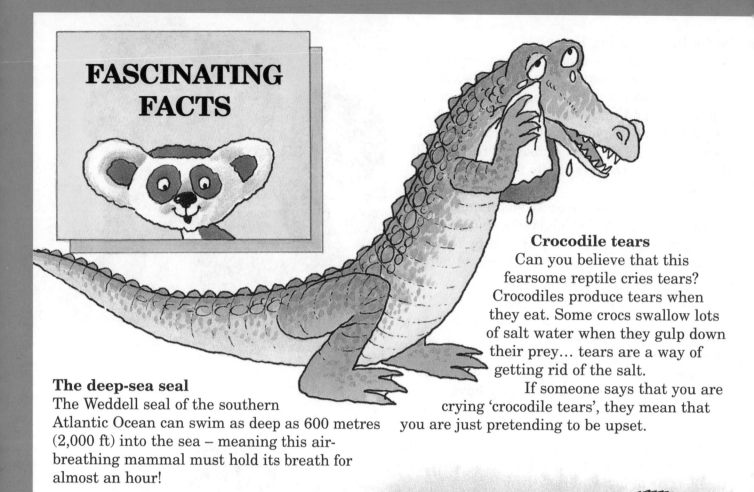

Crocodile tears
Can you believe that this fearsome reptile cries tears? Crocodiles produce tears when they eat. Some crocs swallow lots of salt water when they gulp down their prey… tears are a way of getting rid of the salt.

If someone says that you are crying 'crocodile tears', they mean that you are just pretending to be upset.

The deep-sea seal
The Weddell seal of the southern Atlantic Ocean can swim as deep as 600 metres (2,000 ft) into the sea – meaning this air-breathing mammal must hold its breath for almost an hour!

All change
Everyone knows that a chameleon can change its colour to match its surroundings. This is because the cells of its skin contain colour pigment. When these cells get bigger or smaller, the chameleon's colour changes. These creatures turn particularly colourful when they are hopping mad or courting.

How would you measure up?
The largest of all crustaceans is the Japanese spider crab. Although its average body size is about 30 centimetres (12 in), its legspan measures almost 3.5 metres (12 ft) from the tip of one claw to the other. Compare this with the tiny pea crab that lives inside the shells of mussels and oysters; it really is about the size of a pea and is the smallest crab of all!

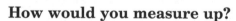

A vegetarian piranha?

Believe it or not, some are! They feed on fruit, leaves and even flowers. Other piranhas, however, are strict meat-eaters. These vicious predators, with their razor-sharp teeth and powerful jaws, will tear flesh to shreds in seconds. They frequently attack and kill large animals. They often attack in groups (called shoals), especially if the water is disturbed... so be sure not to fall off a boat in certain rivers of South America!

Are all piranhas dangerous?

More than a dozen species of piranha exist, but it is believed that only four are dangerous. However, it is probably unwise for you to test whether this is true or not!

Heads or tails?

As piranhas swim along, they often take a bite out of the fins and tails of other fish that happen to be passing by... very nasty! But over a long period of time, one fish has evolved that has solved this problem. A variety of cichlid, rather like a perch, is able to fool the piranha.

Its tail and fins have grown into a shape that resembles its head. It even has a spot on its tail that looks like an eye, so the hungry piranhas can't tell the head from the tail, and therefore leave the cichlid alone. The ferocious fishes must look elsewhere for their snack!

A close shave
Sometimes the Indians of South America use the jaws and sharp teeth of the piranha as razor blades!

THE WONDERFUL WOLF

Wolves rarely attack humans unless they are under threat. Stories of wolves killing people are often exaggerated. But wolves, like all wild dogs, hunt other animals for food.

Over the years, Man has killed wolves because they are a threat to farm animals. Wolves have also declined because the human population has increased.

There are two main types of wolf, the grey wolf and the red wolf (which is now extinct in the wild). Grey wolves are the largest members of the dog family, measuring up to 1 metre (3 ft) high at the shoulder and weighing up to 80 kilograms (176 lb).

Do wolves howl at the moon?
When the howling of wolves echoes through the forest on a moonlit night, it is an eerie, chilling sound! But the wolves aren't really howling at the moon, or getting ready to attack anyone, as some people believe... there is, in fact, a simpler explanation.

They are actually warning other wolves to stay away from their territory. The wolves can often be heard over a distance of 10 kilometres (6 mi). By howling this way, different packs can avoid meeting, which will often lead to fighting and sometimes even death! First the head of the pack begins to howl, then the rest join in the chorus!

Family packs

Wolves are social animals. They live and hunt together and share their food with one another. A pack consists of 8-20 animals (several pairs of wolves and their young), and is led by a dominant male and female pair. Wolves mate for life, and the pack's leading pair breed more often than other pairs in that group. Members of the pack protect each other from enemies.

Leader of the pack

The leader of the pack shows its dominance over the others by snarling and baring its teeth. Wolves that rank lower in the pack flatten their ears and put their tails between their legs to show submission.

Wolf facts

All pet dogs are descended from wolves.

Packs of wolves can bring down large prey like caribou, deer and moose, which may weigh ten times as much as a single wolf.

If a wolf hunts alone or food is scarce, he may eat mice, frogs, insects and berries.

Grey wolves are not always grey. Those living in forests are usually greyish, but wolves ranging the northern Arctic may be white or black, with a pale underside.

Young wolves often play games of chase and tag. Sometimes they will pick up a stick and carry it – just like our pet dogs!

Wolves are good swimmers and often catch fish where the water is shallow.

Female wolves give birth to about seven cubs. In just four months the babies are strong enough to run with the pack.
A wolf may live up to 16 years in the wild, often over 20 in captivity.

ANIMAL ALLSORTS

Calling all beavers!

You may hear a loud smacking sound if you are ever passing by a lake in Canada. It's a warning call, but not for you!

Beavers slap the water with their strong flat tails; this warns other beavers of danger. The loud slapping noise frightens their enemies and tells other beavers to swim for the safety of deeper water.

Let's go to work!

Beavers use their hand-like front paws to eat grasses, bark and twigs. They use their strong front teeth for gnawing down trees – the small trees and twigs are then used to build dams and underwater hideaways.

Beavers also secrete a substance called castoreum which is used as an ingredient in making perfume.

Elephant crocodile

When little children walk in a 'crocodile', they hold each other's hands. When elephants walk in single file, they curve their trunk around the tail of the elephant in front. Walking in a 'crocodile' stops children from getting lost… but it would be difficult to lose an elephant!

Does a turtle need a toothbrush?

No, all living turtles are toothless. As they cannot chew, the turtle uses the sharp edges of its jaw to force small pieces of food down to the stomach.

Who makes a nest on a compost heap?

The American alligator lays its eggs in a nest of rotting vegetation. The eggs are incubated by the heat from the rotting material… just like the compost heap in a garden.

Do wasps collect newspapers?

Luckily, they don't have to! A wasp's nest is constructed of layer upon layer of thin paper walls. The walls are made of chewed-up wood fibres.

Wasps collect tiny scraps of wood from all kinds of places – trees, fence posts, even from old wooden doors and windows… then they start munching! A large wasp's nest can become as big as a football. Sometimes it is multicoloured as the wasps bring many kinds of wood to chew.

Wasps, unlike bees, abandon their nests in autumn and make a new one in spring.

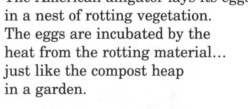

ROAMING THE PLAINS

The American bison, (which in the USA is commonly, though mistakenly, called the 'buffalo'), is now returning from near extinction. Once there were 50 million of them roaming the plains of North America. But by the end of the 1800s less than 1,000 remained. The rest were simply slaughtered by settlers!

Happily the American bison are now coming back. Up to 200,000 animals live on ranches and in parks; over 4,000 range freely in California's Yellowstone National Park.

Little Miracle

Miracle, a very rare white bison calf, was born in the US state of Wisconsin in 1994. The Native Americans believe that this is a sign of great change, and this little calf holds a place of honour among the tribes.

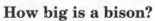

How big is a bison?

A bison can weigh up to 900 kilograms (1,985 lb) and stand at more than 1.9 metres (6 ft). But the biggest buffalo in the world is a 60 ton concrete statue in Jamestown, North Dakota, not far from the National Buffalo Museum.

Hairy head-bangers

When bison bulls fight, hooves pound, dust flies and heads and horns crash together. The fights occasionally end in death, but most of the time bisons only threaten each other.

Can you run as fast as a bison?

You would have to be really speedy! A buffalo can run at over 50 kilometres (30 mi) per hour – that's about three times faster than you can!

Bison or buffalo?

Both bison and buffaloes are members of the cattle family. True buffaloes are only found in southern and eastern Africa. There are two species of bison – the American and the European (called a 'wisent'). Americans commonly refer to their bison as buffalo.

When one howls… they all howl!

Also roaming the North American plains is the coyote, which is similar to the wolf but smaller. It howls to communicate with other coyotes, and they answer back.

Playing dead

The clever coyote is quite an actor. As he lays perfectly still on the ground pretending to be dead, birds that feed on dead animals fly down to investigate. Up jumps the coyote, very much alive, to make a meal of one of them.

Who's that watching from the tree?

The one creature that isn't bothered by the skunk's nasty spray is the great horned owl… it eats skunks! All owls have wings with soft feathers, so they make no sound at all as they sweep down on their prey.

Don't trust a baby skunk

When the skunk is threatened, it turns its back, lifts its tail as a warning, and then sprays its attacker with a foul-smelling scent. Don't trust a baby skunk, it can spray at even one month old!

HOGS, PIGS AND PECCARIES

Pigs come in all sizes and colours – pink, ginger, black, pigs with spots and pigs with dots, little pigs with stripes and even pigs with potbellies!

Pigs in France are trained to track down truffles. Their keen sense of smell quickly finds this valuable fungus which is buried a spade's depth underground, often among the roots of oak trees.

Not a pretty pig!
The wart hog isn't everybody's idea of a beauty, with its big facial warts and whiskered ears!

This African hog grazes on short grass and seeds using its wide lips – its tusks are the wrong shape to dig out food. The wart hog's tassel tail makes a useful fly swatter!

Not a pet piggy!
Large wild boars can weigh a massive 200 kilograms (440 lb)! They will forage through woods and forests for roots, fungi and bulbs. They will sometimes eat mice and frogs and dig up earthworms.

Male boars are armed with razor-sharp tusks. When two rivals fight, they slash at each other's cheeks and stomachs and can inflict terrible wounds.

Wild boar

Going underground!
Wart hogs often seek shelter from danger in aardvark burrows.

Little piggy!
The pygmy hog from Assam in India is the world's smallest pig. You can hold a piglet in the palm of one hand, and the adult is only 30 centimetres (12 in) high.

Pigs don't sweat!
The saying 'to sweat like a pig' is untrue – pigs don't sweat at all! They prefer to wallow in mud – it helps reduce body heat.

Pint-sized pigs

Peccaries are very close relatives of pigs, but a lot smaller in size. Some live in rainforests while others live in hot dry deserts in North and South America.

The collared peccary is very small, around 40 centimetres (16 in) high. When these little pigs are afraid, the white hair on their neck is raised and looks very much like a collar! Their jaws and teeth are strong enough to munch thorny cacti.

Is it a pig or a deer?

The babirusa is a rare wild hog living on Sulawesi and a few nearby islands off Malaysia. Its name means 'pig-deer' because of its four antler-like tusks. Two of them grow backwards in a curve and sometimes touch the hog's forehead!

Is it a bear or a pig?

The African aardvark is known as the 'earth pig', as it resembles a pig, or the 'ant bear', because it lives on ants. In fact, it is neither.

This strange, elusive animal only moves around at night, clawing open termite mounds and licking up the insects with its long sticky tongue.

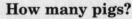

Babirusa

How many pigs?

Nearly half the world's pig population live in China – around a whopping 400 million!

Did you know?

Pigs have been domesticated for almost 5,000 years.

Big piggy!

The biggest pig of all is the African forest hog – weighing in at 275 kilograms (606 lb).

The emperor's decree

Many years ago in ancient China, only the emperor was allowed to eat pork. Sausages and bacon for his royal breakfast... rice for everyone else!

Aardvark

FASCINATING FACTS

Millions of them!
The crab-eating seal
is the most abundant
large mammal on Earth.
Millions live in the Antarctic
among the pack ice... but they
don't eat crabs... they dine on fish
and squid and millions of tons of krill.

A golden tale!
Over 150 years ago a wild golden hamster was
found in Syria.

Almost a century went by before another
one was seen, in 1930. It was a female with
12 babies which were taken to Israel and
encouraged to breed! Now look at the millions
of pet golden hamsters there are all over the
world... what a happy ending!

Kiwi

I smell a worm!
The kiwi of New Zealand hunts at night,
poking into the ground or rotten wood with its
long beak.

It has a very keen sense of smell, which is
rare for birds, and can easily sniff out juicy
earthworms and grubs with nostrils on the tip
of its beak.

Boys or girls?

All boys or all girls, that's the rule for Mum and Dad armadillo!

In the armadillo's family brothers and sisters are never born at the same time. A litter of baby armadillos will always be all-male or else all-female.

A mermaid's purse

When people found this empty case (above) washed up on the beach, they called it a 'mermaid's purse'. The 'purse' contained the egg of a dogfish, which is a small type of shark. When the young dogfish is born, the case is left behind... unless mermaids really are that careless with their purses!

Spooky sounds

If you are sitting in silence in an old house, perhaps with beams or wooden panelling, you might hear an eerie tapping sound – like the ticking of a clock.

Is it a ghost? No, it's probably a death-watch beetle knocking his head against the roof of a tunnel he has bored in the timbers of the house. He's hoping to attract a mate.

Years ago people believed that a person in the house was going to die if they heard the death-watch beetle!

Dogfish

57

PANDAS AND BANDITS

What is a panda?

Firstly, there are two types of panda, the giant panda and the red panda: the giant panda is commonly classified as a bear; the red panda is usually linked with the raccoon family.

When a panda cub is born it is no bigger than a hamster! The tiny cub is blind and helpless at first, with hardly any hair, but its distinctive black markings already show on its pink skin. A baby panda doesn't take its first steps until it is five months old, by then it weighs 25 kilograms (55 lb)... and in another six months its weight will have doubled!

Adult pandas spend up to 16 hours a day eating. The bamboo plant on which they feed has little nourishment, so they must eat up to 45 kilograms (100 lb) of shoots and leaves daily.

Only around a thousand giant pandas survive in the wild, high up in the mountains and bamboo forests of southwest China.

The panda's special paw

Each front paw of the panda has six digits. The extra one is really an enlarged wrist bone that works as an opposite thumb – perfect for grasping tiny bamboo shoots and slender stems.

America's furry bandit

Raccoons are full of mischief, and the black 'face-mask' across their eyes makes them look like a comical bandit!

The common raccoon is widespread across the USA and is no danger of becoming extinct... there are millions of them!

They will eat almost anything, from crayfish to cornflakes. Most farmers consider them a pest as they devour crops. Fruit, vegetables, nothing is safe from raccoons... they even raid hen houses and steal the eggs!

But they can be helpful too, for raccoons eat grubs, grasshoppers, beetles, bugs and mice that can be a nuisance to the farmer.

These clever animals are as happy living near humans as they are roaming the wild. Raccoons can find food anywhere, by raiding dustbins and camp sites and begging for scraps by the roadside. They have very dextrous fingers and can easily open food packets!

Raccoons don't like the cold! In the north, if the temperature drops below -4°C (25°F) for a time, or heavy snows occur, the raccoon falls into a deep sleep for weeks on end. It is not in true hibernation; it just doesn't like winter weather!

The red panda

This small, reddish-brown panda looks like a favourite soft toy! Its weight is at least 20 times less than its relative, the giant panda!

The red panda lives high up in the remote forests of the eastern Himalayas and in southern China. It is nocturnal and spends most of its time climbing trees and feeding on nuts, fruit and bamboo – it has the same special paw as the larger panda.

The young are born and raised in hollow trees or caves. Can you believe the red panda's babies are the same size as giant panda babies when they are born?

BELIEVE IT OR NOT

What an actor!

If the Virginia opossum is in danger, it doesn't always run away. It may throw itself on its back, feet in the air, eyes closed, tongue hanging out and perfectly stiff! The opposum is just 'playing dead'. Its acting is good enough to fool any enemy. When danger is past, the opossum jumps up and runs away... very much alive.

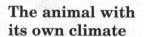

Look who's wearing snow shoes!

The Arctic hare has large fur-coated paws, which work just like snow shoes. The size of the paws help the hare to run across the snow without sinking. In autumn it sheds its brown fur coat and grows a white one, which camouflages the hare in the snow (helping to hide it from its enemy, the Arctic fox).

Beetle brooch

In the 1930s, fashionable ladies who were tired of wearing their jewellery and wanted a change, would attach a fine gold chain to a brilliantly-coloured beetle and tether it to their dress... a living beetle brooch!

The animal with its own climate

Climate conditions are always perfect for Australian hopping-mice. They live in such hot dry conditions that it is almost impossible to find water, so they huddle together during the day in deep burrows, where their warm bodies create moisture – and their very own mini-climate!

What the well-dressed penguin is wearing

Perhaps penguins don't have much of a colour sense, but they do know how to keep nice and warm!

In the ice cold waters surrounding Antarctica, the penguin is kept warm and dry by a dense coat made up of three layers of oily feathers... smart bird!

Crabs live to fight another day

Crabs only have to bump into each other and there's trouble! Two cross crabs are like wrestlers, grabbing and throwing one another around the ring.

When one crab is winning, his opponent simply leaves one of his limbs behind in the other's claws and limps off.

Some beetles stink!

They certainly do! The stink bug from Venezuela really pongs! And it tastes as bad as it smells.

Its disgusting odour and flavour prevent it from being eaten.

A toad that can dig

The spade-foot toad doesn't need a spade at all. He can dig so rapidly with his shovel-shaped hind feet that he can vanish vertically into sandy soil in no time at all.

The bird that could be grounded

If the great bustard puts on a little extra weight, the world's heaviest flying bird could be too big to take off.

Although they are good flyers, great bustards seldom leave the ground, which is not surprising as they can weigh over 22 kilograms (48.5 lb).

Not a tooth in their heads

It doesn't really matter if a turtle or a tortoise is young or old, either way they have no teeth! Sharp edges on their jaws and powerful horny beaks tear their food apart.

Be careful if you paddle in a river or pond in North America, turtles there might snap your toe off... that's why they're called snapping turtles!

A fish with antifreeze!

Many Antarctic fish have special chemicals called glycopeptides that circulate in their blood. This natural antifreeze helps stop the fish from freezing!

MONSTERS, LIZARDS AND DRAGONS

Gila monster

Beware killer monsters!

There are only two lizards in the world that are poisonous: the Gila monster (you might find one if you travel through Death Valley, USA) and the Mexican bearded lizard.

A single bite from either one of these reptiles can be fatal! Their venom glands are in their bottom jaw, and when they bite the deadly poison oozes into the wound and kills.

Keep well away!

The Australian frilled lizard likes to make itself look really scary and much bigger than it is. This frilly lizard is perfectly harmless, but when danger threatens, it can raise the flap of skin around its neck, open its mouth and hiss loudly... looks terrifying doesn't it?

Heads or tails?

The shingle-backed lizard has a shape that would deceive any attacker; its tail looks almost the same as its head... can you tell which end is which?

Australian frilled lizard

Lizards and wings

Some lizards really look as if they can fly. They have very long ribs with flaps of thin skin on either side which they spread out like a parachute. Flying lizards don't really fly, they tend to glide downwards from tree to tree, although they can travel as far as 20 metres (65 ft) in a single glide!

Gecko

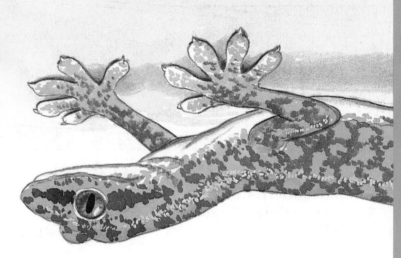

Flying lizard

Look who can walk on the ceiling!

Geckos are amazing climbers. They can run up walls and even walk upside down on the ceiling. The soles of their feet and flat round toes are covered in ridges with thousands of minute projections. They can grip any surface, from a rough tree trunk to a smooth pane of glass. They have no eyelids; they wipe their eyes clean with a lick of their moist tongues.

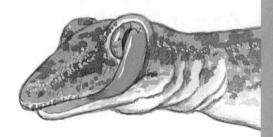

The gigantic Komodo dragon

The world's largest lizard is a hunter as fierce and frightening as it looks. It can kill and eat large animals and often devours deer, wild pigs and horses. It will attack people by biting them severely. It is not unusual for Komodo dragons to kill and eat people too!

This huge lizard is found only on a few islands in Indonesia. Around 5,000 of these reptiles live in a special reserve on Komodo island.

They average about 2.2 metres (7 ft 5 in) in length and weigh approximately 60 kilograms (132 lb).

Komodo dragon

ANIMAL ALLSORTS

Why do some animals hibernate?

In winter, nature tells some animals that it is time to hibernate, or go to sleep.

Food is scarce in cold weather. Trees are bare, there are no fruit or berries and there are very few insects. If all animals were still active in winter, many would starve.

While asleep an animal's body temperature drops and their heartbeat and blood flow slow down, helping to conserve energy.

When they awake in spring, the animals have lost a lot of weight, having lived on their body fat which was stored up during the previous summer. Their first concern is the search for food, which becomes plentiful as the weather grows warmer.

How many fleas?

Did you know that a little hedgehog has about 5,000 spines in its coat, and up to 500 fleas?!

These are hedgehog fleas, which rarely bite humans... what a relief!

Which cat has paws like a dog?

The cheetah. Unlike all other cats, it cannot pull in its claws.

Do mammals breathe air?

Yes. Even whales, dolphins and porpoises have to come up to the surface of the water to breathe.

Is this a warning?

If you see a spotted skunk doing handstands, don't stand around watching the performance – just run!

This means that it suspects danger and is about to spray the foulest smelling liquid, and it has a very good aim!

Beware bulldog!

The most dangerous ant in the world is the bulldog ant, found throughout Australia. This huge ant, which measures up to 4 centimetres (1.6 in) long, grips victims with its long jaws while injecting a sting which can kill an adult in a matter of minutes.

The bulldog ant is extremely aggressive and determined... that's how it got its name!

Name the only beetle with a long neck!

Yes, you've guessed it, the giraffe beetle! It's a weevil from Madagascar that has a long giraffe-shaped neck.

Other beetles may have jaws, but only the giraffe beetle has a long neck!

What does a mosquito like to drink?

Coffee, tea, cola? Not at all! A mosquito drinks animal or human blood which it sucks through a needle-like part of its mouth. Rather like drinking through a straw!

Do seals have ears?

Seals do have ears, but they don't have ear flaps like we do. On each side of their head they have a small hole which leads to their 'inner ear'. Eared seals are a different species.

Name that seal!

Species include the oddly-named elephant seal, the leopard seal and the most common seal: the crabeater.

How many eggs does an ostrich lay?

About 12. A female ostrich lays one egg every other day during the breeding season.

How many eggs are in an ostrich's nest?

Often five or six female birds lay their eggs in one gigantic nest which sometimes contains up to 60 eggs... what a huge omelette that would make!

How many wings does a butterfly have?

A butterfly has four wings, two at the front and two at the back. Some of the larger butterflies can use their wings to glide.

How did the rabbit reach Australia?

Around 1860, an English family who went to settle in Australia took with them 24 rabbits (perhaps they thought they would miss these soft furry creatures!).

Today a female rabbit can produce five families in one year. There are usually five or six babies per litter... but there can be as many as 12. As soon as a young female rabbit is just three months old it is able to produce young... so it's not surprising that rabbits very soon became a pest in Australia!

Which insect makes the loudest noise?

The male cicada. This noisy insect 'sings' to attract a mate. It even has a special chamber in its body that amplifies the sound, which can be heard up to 40 kms (25 mi) away.

A garden full of cicadas can make more noise than a pneumatic drill. Luckily the female cicada doesn't sing.

Who has the fastest wing beat?

Although tiny insects beat their wings very fast, they fly slowly. The buzzing noise they make is caused by the beating of their wings. The faster an insect flies, the higher the note of the 'buzz'. The prize for the fastest wing beat goes to a tiny midge whose wings beat over 1,000 times per second... you may hear it, but can you see it?

Who can look both ways at once?

The chameleon. Its large prominent eyes can turn 180°, and each eye can swivel round in a different direction.

Do wasps make honey?

No, they rear their larvae on a diet of chewed up insects and caterpillars. They don't need to collect nectar.

Dentist's delight!

Would you like 52 teeth? Probably not when you go to the dentist! An average human has about 32 teeth.

The numbat from Australia has more teeth than any other land mammal, although it doesn't need them for eating.

This is the only marsupial that feeds purely on termites – up to 20,000 a day – which it licks up with its long sticky tongue. The numbat's 52 tiny teeth are used only for carrying nesting materials. It is an endangered species and survives in small areas of forest in Western Australia.

What is a mammal?

Mammals are warm-blooded animals with spines. Their bodies stay the same temperature whether it is hot or cold.

They give birth to live young which feed on their mother's milk. All of them breathe air.

Elephants, whales, bears, bats and humans are all mammals.

Do any mammals lay eggs?

As a general rule mammals give birth to live young, but there are some exceptions who lay eggs.

Can you guess how many out of some 4,500 different mammals in the world do lay eggs? A thousand, 200, 20? No, it is much lower than that – it's just three! The platypus and the short-beaked echidna of Australia, and the long-beaked echidna of New Guinea. These three animals are monotremes – their young are hatched from soft-shelled eggs.

MAGNIFICENT MACAWS

Macaws can be seen, and their noisy squawking heard, in zoos all over the world. For years, these beautiful birds have been taken from their habitats and sold as pets.

Now wild macaws are becoming rare. The clearing of forests for timber and farming means that space for many animals, birds and plants is dwindling all the time.

Europeans have had pet macaws as early as the 16th century, when they were taken home by Spanish and Portuguese explorers.

Macaws can live up to 60 years in captivity; a few have lived to be over 70! In the wild they reach the age of 35-45.

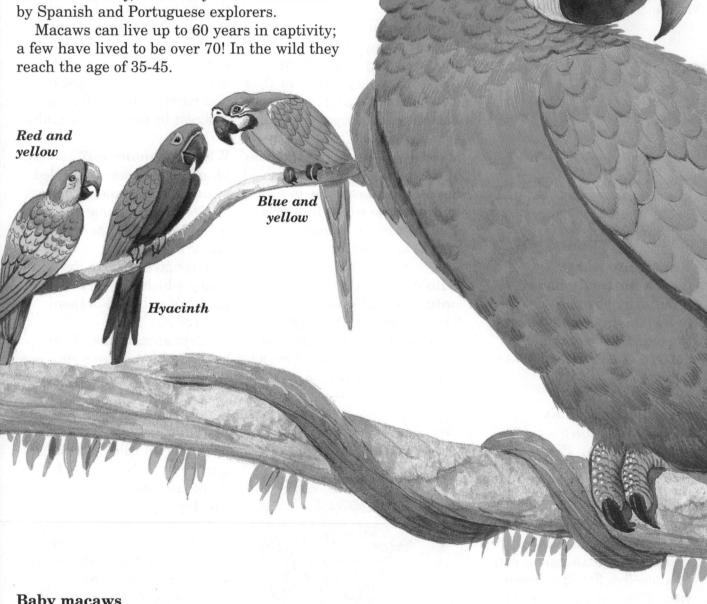

Scarlet macaw

Red and yellow

Hyacinth

Blue and yellow

Baby macaws
Only two eggs are laid by the female bird, but usually only one chick survives. At three to four months old, a young macaw is the same size as its parents and ready to fly. By now its wingspan measures a metre! After just a few days, the young bird is no longer fluttering from branch to branch, but flying high above the forest canopy with Mum and Dad.

Red in the face!
When macaws are agitated or anxious, the featherless part of their face turns bright red. This fades as soon as they calm down.

Giants of the parrot world

The brilliantly coloured macaw is the world's largest parrot. It is found only in Central and South America. Macaws make their nests over 30.4 metres (100 ft) off the ground, high up in the tall slender trees of the rainforest.

There are 16 different species of macaw. At least half of them are more than a metre long from beak to tail.

Is this the world's rarest bird?

The spix macaw is probably the rarest bird of all. Only one survivor is known in the wild (although there are 31 in captivity). People searching for the spix found just one male living deep in the forest of northeast Brazil.

All the colours of the rainbow!

Macaws come in many colours. As well as the scarlet macaw – bright red with yellowish green and blue wings – there is the green military macaw and the bright blue hyacinth to name but a few.

The nutcracker bird

The macaw has the most powerful bite of any bird in the entire world... so watch your fingers!

Its sharp-edged beak can crack open the hardest nut with ease. Macaws usually bite through the pulp of fruit as quickly as possible to get to the seed or stone in the middle.

When feeding, a macaw uses its foot almost like a hand. Two of its claws face forward and two face backwards, which makes gripping fruit really easy.

These agile birds can keep a tight hold of branches with one foot and reach sideways to pick food with the other... they can hang upside down too!

Did you know?

• Toucans are a real threat to macaws. They stick their huge beaks into nest holes and steal an egg or a chick.

• Macaws mate for life. They can be seen flying together in pairs within a flock.

• The first known sighting of a wild blue-throated macaw was in 1992, in Bolivia. Only about 30 of these birds are thought to be in existence.

• Some species once originated from the West Indies too, but now these beautiful birds are extinct there.

FASCINATING FACTS

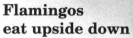

Flamingos eat upside down

It's true. When a flamingo wants food, it places its head and bill upside down in the water. It uses its tongue to force muddy water through the sharp edges of the bill, which strains the water – leaving behind edible material for the flamingo to munch.

Sausages overhead!

The African driver ant is known as the 'sausage fly'... I think you can see why!

Vegetarian vulture

Believe it or not, there is a vegetarian vulture! The palm-nut vulture does not eat meat, which is unusual for a vulture. Instead it enjoys the fruit of the oil-palm, with perhaps a little fish on the side!

Giant panda

What is it?

Europeans and North Americans knew nothing of the giant panda until 1869, when French naturalist Pére David described it on his return from China. It was not until 1937, when one of these lovable creatures was brought over from the East, that Westerners saw a live panda for the first time.

Today pandas are under threat – humans have encroached on their living space, and the bamboo on which they feed may not always be plentiful due to the plant's life cycle. The Chinese government has taken steps to protect the panda, by providing special reserves.

Keeping out the cold

Warm-blooded creatures need to keep their body temperature constant.

When the weather is very cold, birds puff out their feathers and animals fluff up their fur.

A layer of air is trapped next to their skin which helps to keep them warm.

Breakfast is served

The electric eel can stun and even kill fish and frogs with an electric shock from its body.

The eel can emit up to 600 volts – that's more than enough electricity to light a chandelier or make a slice of toast. How shocking!

EXCITING EAGLES

• Eagles have very keen eyesight – four times better than humans.

• A golden eagle can spot its prey over 2 kilometres (1.2 mi) away!

Harpy eagle

The harpy
This fearsome eagle carries away macaws, parrots, sloths and snakes. It can swoop down through the tropical rainforest at 70 kilometres per hour (43 mph), grabbing poor howler monkeys straight off the branches! The harpy is the heaviest of eagles, weighing up to 8 kilograms (18 lb).

The bald eagle
From this... it takes a chick up to six years to acquire his adult plumage.

To this... the symbol of the United States of America.

Thanks to breeding programmes and strict conservation laws, the bald eagle is slowly recovering from the brink of extinction. These creatures build gigantic nests – one such structure measured 6 metres (20 ft) deep and 3 metres (10 ft) wide!

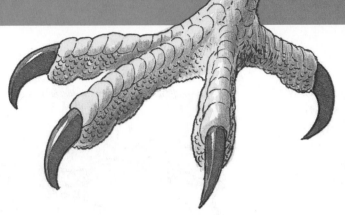

The mighty claw

Eagles have strong talons that are curved to kill and carry their prey through the air. Grip pads or rough patches underneath their feet help them to hold onto the prey. They grasp the meal with their talons and tear up the meat with their sharp beaks.

Did you know?

• The bald eagle was chosen as the national bird of the USA in 1782.
• The African fish eagle kills flamingos as well as fish.
• Eagle chicks often take several days to come out of their shells.
• The African martial eagle is strong enough to fly off with a small antelope or goat; it has a wingspan of 2 metres (6.5 ft).
• The pallas fishing eagle can carry up to 6 kilograms (13 lb) in weight.
• The rare Philippine eagle is the world's tallest eagle at 1 metre (39 in) high. Its favourite prey is flying lemurs.

The eagle and the sea snake

Sea snakes are among the most poisonous snakes in the world, but the white-bellied sea eagle has no difficulty catching them, and comes to no harm.

From high in the sky, the eagle spots the deadly snake as it comes to the surface to breathe. Swiftly the eagle swoops down and grabs the sea snake, killing it with its powerful talons, then taking it to its nest.

Acrobats of the sky

The bateleur eagle's name means 'tumbler' in French. As they fly, male bateleurs perform spectacular aerobatics, often using their amazing flying skills to harass other birds into dropping their prey.

The bateleur spends most of its time in the air and may fly over 320 kilometres (200 mi) per day while hunting.

Birds use their tails as rudders, but these eagles have virtually no tail, so they must constantly tilt their wings during flight.

BELIEVE IT OR NOT

How much can a camel drink?
If a camel is really thirsty and has gone a long time without water, it can drink up to 180 litres (40 gallons) of water in less than 20 minutes... that's about 20 full buckets!

Can a vulture sing?
Not a note! Vultures hiss, grunt and growl... they are definitely not one of nature's songbirds!

The duck with a duvet
The eider duck builds a nest and lines it with its own soft downy feathers.

People collect eiderdown to fill duvets and jackets; it's one of the best natural materials to keep out the cold.

What makes an adder madder?
That prickly creature, the hedgehog! They attack adders, but the snake's venom doesn't harm the hedgehog one bit – it is resistant to it.

How fast can you lick a lolly?
Not as fast as a hummingbird. They can lick nectar from flowers with their lightning tongues at 13 times a second!

The killer whale is really a dolphin
Its name sounds like a whale and this mammal looks like a whale, but the killer whale, or orca, is the biggest of all the dolphins.

Which insects have the biggest eyes?

Dragonflies. They need good eyesight as they hunt and catch other insects while flying. Their eyes are made up of thousands of different lenses which give the dragonfly an accurate view in different directions.

Taking a bath without water

Some animals and birds don't take baths as we do... they prefer a dust-bath.

The dust helps keep feathers in good condition and removes stubborn parasites that cling to furry or feathery coats.

A pretty pink walrus!

When a walrus is stretched out in the sun, it can turn quite pink! But this isn't a sunburn. It's the result of blood flowing to the surface of the walrus's skin, in order to absorb heat from the sun's warm rays. The pink colour fades when the walrus returns to the sea.

The fish with the saw nose

Although the sawfish looks as if it could cut a shark in half, it doesn't!

It thrashes its saw-shaped nose from side to side to kill or stun a small fish, or disturb sea creatures by raking its 'saw' along the sea bed.

Can music really 'charm' snakes?

Certainly not, as snakes are deaf! They are 'charmed' by the movement of the snake-charmer's pipe. The snake moves from side to side because it's preparing to strike.

THE ANTARCTIC EMPEROR

Antarctica is the coldest place on Earth, with biting, icy winds and blizzards that blow for days on end, temperatures that can fall as low as -80°C and a sea that's frozen over for most of the year.

Despite this harsh environment, a number of animals and birds are able to live and breed here. The emperor penguin even chooses the dark depths of the Antarctic winter to rear its young on the open pack ice. These hardy penguins gather together in colonies of a few hundred to 60,000; they return year after year to the same spot. In spite of the bitterly cold conditions, emperor penguins usually live for up to 20 years.

Penguins don't walk very well, they waddle or hop. They find that 'tobogganing' is a much easier way to travel – although it is rather slow! The birds slither along on their tummies, propelled across the ice by their clawed webbed feet. They often travel up to 80 kilometres (50 mi) this way!

The empress
The female penguin lays just one white egg each year in May. She then returns to the sea for two months to feed, leaving her partner to incubate the egg on his own for up to 60 days. The male stands perfectly still on the ice in the endless darkness of winter, with the egg balanced on the tops of his feet and tucked snugly beneath soft downy feathers. There is also a special area of bare skin (a brood patch), at the bottom of the penguin's body to keep the egg warm.

The little emperor
When the egg hatches, the female returns. Now it's Dad's turn to go off to sea and find food... as he has lost up to half his body weight!

The female keeps her chick warm and well fed on regurgitated seafood for the first two months. Then the little emperor penguins are left during the day in a 'penguin creche' with hundreds of others, while the adults go off to find food. Each chick can recognise its own parents by their call when they return, and waddles towards them at once.

The emperor

Of the 17 different types of penguin, the emperor is by far the biggest, standing at almost 1.2 metres (4 ft) tall and weighing about 32 kilograms (70 lb).

When hunting for fish and squid, these penguins can dive to a depth of over 450 metres (1,476 ft), and they can stay underwater up to 18 minutes. They swim to the surface so quickly, they often shoot as high as 2 metres (6.5 ft) above the water.

WHAT STRANGE BEHAVIOUR!

What a song and dance!

Crowned cranes put on a spectacular display when looking for a mate. Dancing, and even singing duets, helps them to choose a partner.

First, the male crowned crane bows to a female, leaping in front of her until she joins in the dance. Next the couple stretch out their wings and strut around each other in a circle, diving towards one another, then leaping apart. Finally they spring up into the air – often as high as 6 metres (20 ft)!

Crowned cranes in action

Listen, it's a talking egg!

Sometimes baby alligators and crocodiles make such a noise while still in their eggs. They do it when they're ready to hatch. They tap from inside their shells, or make soft grunting noises that can be heard by other youngsters who are about to hatch too!

A clown's sleeping bag

There is a small fish found in tropical coral reefs that can hide, rest and sleep in complete safety among the stinging tentacles of the sea anemone.

The brightly coloured clown fish coats its body with a special mucus which counteracts the anemone's poison. It is perfectly protected in its very own 'sleeping bag', quite safe from ocean predators!

A fur coat that eats moths!

Some greedy grizzlies in Yellowstone National Park, USA, climb up the mountains for a summertime feast.

Millions of moths migrate from the Great Plains to feed on the nectar of alpine flowers that grow in the mountains. Many of the park bears clamber up to gorge themselves all day long on these tasty moths, scooping up thousands with their tongues. Eating so many of these nutritious insects helps them gain a layer of fat for the winter.

A monkey making snowballs?

Japanese macaques living in northern Japan experience winters that are harsh with heavy falls of snow. Luckily they have thick hairy coats which protect them from the worst of the weather.

The younger macaques are often seen making snowballs, rolling them along the ground just like children do when they play in the snow!

Although these monkeys make snowballs and carry them around, no-one has ever seen them throw one!

Beat out that rhythm on the drum!

The Australian palm cockatoo likes to be heard when he goes courting. First he finds a twig that is just the right size for a drumstick, then he bangs it on a hollow log... a special drum solo performed for the female palm cockatoo of his choice!

BIRDS AND BEAKS

Birds' beaks come in many shapes and sizes. In fact, you can tell which foods a bird eats by looking at the shape of its beak.

Some birds sip nectar from flowers while others feed on meat and fish. There are birds that peck seeds or crack shells, a few can sieve food from water and mud; many crunch insects and beetles.

Around the world there are 8,800 different kinds of birds, and every species has the perfect beak to find the food it needs to survive – from the tearing beak of the bald eagle to the gaping beak of the common nighthawk.

Frigate birds
These hooked-bill creatures snatch food from the sea with ease. Shown right is a male displaying for a female by blowing up its throat pouch.

Frigate bird

Vulture

Vultures
These particularly vicious birds of prey use their powerful beaks with hooked ends to rip up chunks of meat.

Hornbill

Hornbills
The hornbill's chunky beak grows over its head to form a helmet. These birds use their strong beaks to pick fruit and crack the tough shells of nuts they find in the rainforest.

Hornbills mate for life. When the female is ready to lay eggs, the couple finds a hollow tree and plasters round the nest hole – using their huge beaks as trowels.

Once the female is inside, the male hornbill seals up the nest, just leaving a small slit through which he passes her regurgitated food with his beak.

This routine may last up to three months, until the eggs have hatched and the young birds have grown.

78

Hummingbirds

The world's smallest bird is the bee hummingbird from Cuba. This tiny creature is no bigger than some moths – measuring just under 6 centimetres (2.2 in) from beak to tail and weighing a mere 1.6 grams (0.056 oz).

The sword-billed hummingbird from South America has a 10 centimetre (4 in) bill – almost half its total length!

The beaks of hummingbirds are specially shaped to reach deep down into flowers. This way they can sip nectar with their tongues (which can stretch to twice the length of their beak!).

Spoonbills

This water bird swings its long, flat-ended bill from side to side sieving the water for food. The instant it touches a fish, or perhaps a crab, its spoon-shaped bill snaps shut and the food is swallowed.

Parrot

Parrots

These colourful feathered friends have beaks that are short, strong and curved – just right for cracking those tasty nuts and seeds with tough shells!

Avocet

Avocets

An avocet feeds on small aquatic creatures, which it catches by swishing its slender upturned bill from side to side through the water.

Oystercatchers

This sea bird's bill is shaped like a knife blade, and is used with great success to prise open shellfish and lever limpets from the rocks.

Oystercatcher

Spoonbill

Crossbill

Crossbills

The top and bottom of the crossbill's beak cross over so the bird can easily dig out seeds from pine cones.

BELIEVE IT OR NOT

The cat with furry slippers

If you meet a sand cat as you travel across the desert, you might think it's wearing furry slippers.

Sand cats have thick fur padding between their toes, which stops them from sinking into the soft sand and protects their paws from burning.

No earmuffs for this fox

The Arctic fox has short rounded ears, much smaller than other foxes. This ear shape conserves precious body heat in the bitterly cold polar climate. If his ears were larger, heat would escape, then he would really need earmuffs!

The deadly seashell!

The cone shell holds one of the most poisonous creatures in the sea – its paralysing venom can kill within hours. An empty cone shell, however, is very beautiful and much prized by collectors.

A fishy tail

The USA's biggest cat loves fish for tea! The jaguar often wades into a lake or river and carefully swishes his tail about. When the fish rise to the surface to investigate, they are scooped up in the jaguar's paws and swiftly eaten.

The longest silken thread

Many caterpillars produce silk when spinning a cocoon, but only the mulberry silkworm spins 1.2 kilometres (3,900 ft) of silk in one single thread!

See-through wings

Butterflies have two pairs of wings. The vibrant colours of their wings are produced by thousands of scales that catch the light. Some butterflies and moths have almost clear wings because they have so few scales – which makes it harder for their enemies to see them.

80

Can a seal blow up a balloon?

When a hooded seal is feeling aggressive, he fills the lining of his nostrils with air, and looks just like a bright red balloon. Not content with that, he can also inflate his nasal cavity, and look just like a black balloon!

Can you prick your finger on a beetle?

There is a beetle, the tree-hopper, that looks just like a rose thorn, but it won't prick your finger!

This insect has the most amazing shape, resembling parts of plants and flowers.

The bird with no nest

The fairy tern of Hawaii builds no nest at all. Its single egg is balanced on a bare branch or in the fork of two small branches.

Luckily the tern's chick has long sharp claws to help it cling on!

What a bouncing baby

A baby pygmy hippopotamus weighs about the same as a human baby at birth, usually about 4 kilograms (9 lb). But the offspring of the familiar common hippo is a real bouncing baby, weighing in at a whopping 42 kilograms (93 lb)... now that really is a big baby!

Volcanic bunny

The volcanic rabbit lives on the sides of a volcanic mountain range very close to Mexico City in Central America; it is one of the world's smallest and rarest bunnies.

THE FLIGHTLESS BIRDS

Cassowary

Kiwi

PPP-Penguins!

The most common flightless bird is the penguin. Its wings are no good for flying, but they are fine flippers for propelling through water. Penguins are covered in soft feathers which give them a smooth, sleek line – perfect for swimming!

Kiwi

The kiwi lives in dense forest in New Zealand. It waddles around during the night hunting for worms with its long beak. This hen-sized bird lays an egg 25 per cent of its body weight.

Cassowary

The cassowary really is a bird in a crash helmet! The bony cap on its head is thought to protect the cassowary as it crashes through the undergrowth.

This huge bird can swallow vast quantities of large fruit whole, which it gobbles up from the forest floor. Cassowaries can be very dangerous. One kick from its sharp 12 centimetre (5 in) claw can be deadly.

Rhea   *Ostrich*   *Cassowary*   *Emu*

Ostrich

Ostrich
The ostrich lives wild in Africa. Its wing feathers are soft plumes and useless for flying. If an ostrich is in any danger it can escape at a speedy 70 kilometres (43 mi) per hour.

Emu
The world's second largest flightless bird is the emu. It is found only in Australia and is the country's national bird. Emus can travel up to 45 kilometres (28 mi) per hour, and they can swim too!

Emu

Kakapo
The kakapo, a rare ground parrot from New Zealand, lives in a burrow. It makes a loud booming noise at night which can be heard over 5 kilometres (3 mi) away.

Kakapo

Rhea

Rhea
There are two species of rhea, found in South America – the common rhea and Darwin's rhea. They live in tall grasses and feed on plants and insects. They can easily outrun a horse.

Takahe   *Takahe*
The New Zealand takahe is about 60 centimetres (2 ft) tall. It was thought to be extinct until a few were found in 1948.

WHAT?
WHERE?
WHY?

Why does a cat arch its back?

When a cat is annoyed or afraid, it arches its back and the ridge of hair along its spine stands up.

This acts as a warning signal to enemies, but when a cat's tail is swished from side to side and fluffed out like a bottlebrush, beware, this cat is very cross indeed!

How is a snake able to smell?

With its tongue, of course! Snakes stick their tongues in the air or on the ground to pick up scents.

When a snake's tongue darts back in its mouth, it touches the sensitive lining of the roof. That tells the snake's brain what is nearby... it could be a tasty snack or a dangerous enemy!

Can you catch a fly?

Thought not! A fly has eyes that can look in many directions at the same time. They are very sensitive to movement and react far faster than human eyes.

What is a fledgling?

A very young bird whose feathers have grown enough for it to fly for the first time.

How does a fly walk on the ceiling?

With the sticky pads on its feet. The pads enable it to walk on any surface without falling off.

Why do cats have whiskers?

Cats are hunters – and often in the dark. Whiskers give cats an extra sense of touch, so Kitty can detect early on if any obstacles are in the way.

Can a starfish grow a new limb?

A starfish with one arm shorter than the rest means it has lost a limb and is growing a new one. This could take up to a year.

Which bat can walk on the ground?

The only bat that can do this is the vampire bat... so watch those toes if you're wearing sandals!

What is a raptor?

A raptor is a bird of prey that hunts in daylight. A hawk or a buzzard is a raptor, so is a falcon or an eagle. An owl is not, because it hunts at night.

Why do hippos yawn?

When hippos yawn, they're really showing their teeth! They do this to threaten and frighten off male rivals.

Why do crocodiles yawn?

Perhaps they are bored waiting for their next meal! Not at all! They are opening their jaws as wide as they can to lose heat quickly, especially when basking in the hot sun.

Can hedgehogs climb?

Everyone thinks of the hedgehog as a spiky little animal that scurries through fallen leaves, or scampers across your lawn at night.

But hedgehogs don't always stay so close to the ground... they can easily climb over a 2 metre (6.5 ft) high wire fence, and even dig underneath if they want to reach food!

Why do cats purr?

When a cat is happy and feeling affectionate, it scrapes its vocal cords to produce a purring sound.

Can crabs climb trees?

The robber crab can! This enormous crab is the world's largest and heaviest crustacean living on land. It weighs about 2.5 kilograms (5 lb 8 oz) and has incredibly powerful pincers.

Also known as the coconut crab, it climbs up the trunks of palm trees with ease and snaps off the young coconuts which fall to the floor.

Then it hurries down to the ground and, using its strong pincers, drills a hole in the nuts and scrapes out the flesh. Makes a change from the usual crab diet of small fish and worms!

Crabs have the strangest relations!

You would expect a crab to be the cousin of a crayfish, lobster or prawn! But this claw-wielding crustacean is, in fact, related to the woodlouse – which most people think is an insect!

How high can a flea jump?

The flea can jump as high as 200 millimetres (10 in), which is 130 times its own height. That's the equivalent of you jumping almost as high as the Eiffel Tower!

When is a pig a rodent?

When it is a guinea pig! These small, furry creatures are not pigs, they belong to the rodent family. Today, many homes in the UK have them as pets.

One hump or two?

The bactrian camel, which is found in Central Asia, has two humps. The dromedary camel of the Middle East has only one. Contrary to popular belief the humps store fat, not water.

A dangerous male?

Why is the Australian funnel-web spider different from other poisonous spiders? Because it is the bite of the male that is deadly. In every other species of killing spider... it is the female's bite that can be fatal!

What a lot of eggs!

The female sea turtle lays an incredible 80-180 eggs in one batch (called a 'clutch'). Her eggs are deposited in the sand over a period of ten days to a month... now that's a lot of eggs!

On the roof of the world!

Would you believe it? High-flying bar-headed geese have been seen winging their way over the Himalayas, flapping their wings at a dizzying height of some 9,000 metres (29,520 ft).

AUSTRALIA'S LONG-JUMPER

How big is a kangaroo?
The red kangaroo is the world's largest marsupial. Large males stand as tall as a man and weigh up to 90 kilograms (198 lb). They measure up to 2.4 metres (8 ft) long from nose to tail (which alone measures over one metre).

Are all kangaroos the same?
No, there are about 60 different kinds living in Australia, from the larger kangaroos and wallabies to the smallest of them all, the tiny musky rat kangaroo – which is less than 33 centimetres (13 in) long from nose to tail and weighs only about 500 grams (1 lb).

Tree-kangaroo

Is this a record?
The highest speed ever recorded for a kangaroo was 64 kilometres (40 mi) per hour, by the eastern grey kangaroo.

The record for the high-jump is also held by an eastern grey, which cleared a 2.4 metre (8 ft) fence upon hearing the sound of a car backfiring!

What if a kangaroo gets too hot?
In extremely hot regions, kangaroos rest in the shade during the day and graze at night.

They don't sweat, instead they lick their paws, arms and chests. As the wet saliva evaporates, it cools the blood near the surface of the skin.

Kangaroos have a very thick fur coat, which keeps out the heat as well as the cold!

Can kangaroos climb trees?
The tree-kangaroo is an agile climber who is often mistaken for a monkey (impossible in Australia – monkeys don't live there!).

Unlike other kangaroos, the tree-kangaroo has well-developed front legs – it can hop and walk. They weigh about 13 kilograms (28 lb) and can jump onto the ground from as high as 30 metres (98 ft), always landing upright... then off they bound again!

Why do kangaroos have such long tails?

When kangaroos are hopping along at speed their hind legs swing backwards and forwards – and their tails act as a balance. Their tails are very strong and muscular to support the kangaroo as it hops along.

What is a marsupial?

Koalas, wombats and kangaroos are all marsupials – they give birth to young that develop inside a pouch. The gestation period is relatively short - between 27 and 40 days.

A new-born kangaroo weighs under 1 gram (.035 oz) and is only 3 centimetres (1.2 in) long. The tiny 'joey' climbs into its mother's pouch where it is fed on milk for about 11 months, at which time it is able to hop around. If frightened or tired, a young kangaroo simply pops back into the pouch!

What is a macropod?

The word means 'great-footed animal' – like the kangaroo or wallaby. Macropods all have long feet and powerful hind legs which do not move alternately... that is why kangaroos hop and most can't walk or run!

Can kangaroos box?

The males lock arms and wrestle rather than box. They try to kick box and push each other onto the ground.

BELIEVE IT OR NOT

Can you hear a parrotfish squawk underwater?

No, you can't! The parrotfish was given a bird-like name because of its brilliant colouring and its beak-shaped mouth, not because it squawks!

Parrotfish break off pieces of coral with their strong teeth and destroy great stretches of coral reef.

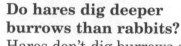

The badger gives the fox a home

The badger isn't being generous, it has no choice!

Too lazy to dig its own den, the cunning fox tries to turn the badger out of its hole. If the poor badger is unwilling to go, the fox sprays the den with foul-smelling liquid from its scent glands. Badgers hate bad smells and will move out at once – giving the sly fox a brand new home.

Do hares dig deeper burrows than rabbits?

Hares don't dig burrows at all! They live out in the open, not together in warrens like their rabbit cousins.

Hares rest in long grass or shallow dips in the ground. Both adults and young (leverets) alike can keep perfectly still, which helps to keep them safe from predators.

A stone house for a mouse

This may sound like a fairy tale, but it's true! The tiny pebble-mouse from Western Australia piles pebbles into mounds. It lives in tunnels under the stone mounds which can cover up to 9 square metres (10 sq yds).

Lions love to hunt!

Not quite, they much prefer resting in the sun, playing with the cubs and waiting for their meals. The lionesses do most of the hunting!

When dinner does arrive, the male lions push the females out of the way and eat first... what remains is for the lionesses and the cubs.

A man can stand on an ostrich egg

This huge egg can easily support the weight of an adult, even though the shell is only 1.5 millimetres (0.06 in) thick!

Polar bears love sliding

Female polar bears go into their snow-drift dens in November to have their cubs. When they come out in March, they roll in the snow and slide down the icy slopes, looking as if they're pleased to be outside again!

All snakes are poisonous

Many snakes are completely harmless, only about 15 per cent are venomous. Make sure you know which they are!

Only male deer have antlers

As a general rule this is true, but there is one exception. A female caribou (or reindeer) has a set of antlers... just ask Father Christmas!

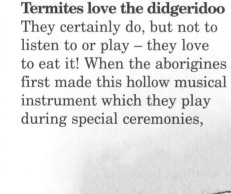

Termites love the didgeridoo

They certainly do, but not to listen to or play – they love to eat it! When the aborigines first made this hollow musical instrument which they play during special ceremonies,

they would find a straight branch of eucalyptus tree and bury it in a termite's mound. The termites would eat the soft wood in the middle, leaving a hollow tube ready to be played.

KOALAS AND WOMBATS

As the koala looks rather like a soft cuddly bear, it is often wrongly called 'the koala bear'. In fact, it is not a bear at all; the koala's closest relative is the wombat.

Millions of years ago these two animals shared a common ancestor. The koala, like the wombat, is a marsupial – an animal with a pouch. A female koala has just one baby, which is less than two centimetres long and weighs only half a gram! The bee-sized baby climbs into its mother's pouch where it develops for about six months, until it is strong enough to climb onto its mother's back. A young koala is at least a year old before it ventures off on its own.

There are three kinds of wombat – the common wombat, the southern hairy-nosed wombat and the northern hairy-nosed wombat (of which there are only 100 left). The common wombat has a bare nose!

Watch out for wombats!

This road sign warns motorists to watch out for wombats in areas where they cross the road. Over a short distance a wombat can run at 40 kilometres (25 mi) per hour.

Wombats are one of the largest burrowing animals in the world. During the night they get really busy! With their strong claws, they can dig out 2 metres (6.5 ft) of tunnel by morning. Their burrows are a maze of corridors often 30 metres (100 ft) long, opening up into sleeping areas lined with leaves, grass and twigs. Generations of wombats have often lived in the same burrows, which on occasion help keep them safe from bushfires.

Wombat

In the beginning...
A new-born wombat is as small as a bean. This tiny baby stays in its mother's pouch for up to seven months. When the young wombat becomes an adult, it can weigh between 20-40 kilograms (44-88 lb).

Clever Wombie!
Wombats have highly developed brains, and are by far the cleverest of all the marsupials. They learn quickly and are playful creatures.

Under threat
Koalas are threatened by the loss of eucalyptus trees; the animals are now protected by law.

Feeding time
The main diet of a koala is leaves of the eucalyptus tree in which it lives. These leaves are low in protein and produce little energy. This is why adult koalas spend about four hours a day eating, and up to 20 hours sleeping – so much dozing helps conserve energy!

Did you know?

• There are two 'thumbs' and three 'fingers' on a koala's front paws which, together with strong sharp claws, make the koala a great climber.

• Male koalas are up to 50 per cent heavier than females.

• The koala will curl up tightly into a ball to keep warm, and will spread out to keep cool.

• A koala does have a tail, but to see it you have to look very closely.

• During the mating season male koalas make a lot of noise. Their loud bellows and growls echo through the forest at night.

• The koala has a distinctive smell, rather like a cough sweet! It picks up this scent from the eucalyptus trees in which it lives. This strong odour keeps irritating parasites at bay that would otherwise live in the koala's thick fur.

Koala and baby

INDEX

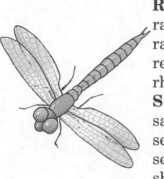

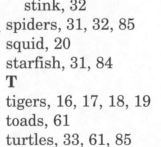
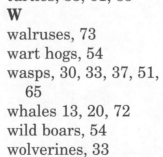